1 MONTH OF
FREE
READING

at

www.ForgottenBooks.com

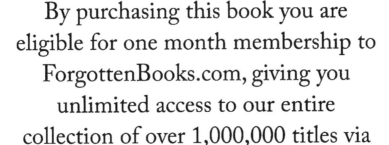

By purchasing this book you are eligible for one month membership to ForgottenBooks.com, giving you unlimited access to our entire collection of over 1,000,000 titles via our web site and mobile apps.

To claim your free month visit:

www.forgottenbooks.com/free45299

ISBN 978-1-5281-5411-6
PIBN 10045299

𝔘nited 𝔖tates 𝔠atholic 𝔥istorical 𝔖ociety

Diary of a Visit

TO THE

United States of America

IN THE YEAR 1883

BY

CHARLES LORD RUSSELL OF KILLOWEN

Late Lord Chief Justice of England

WITH AN INTRODUCTION BY THE

REV. MATTHEW RUSSELL, S.J.

AND

AN APPENDIX BY

THOMAS FRANCIS MEEHAN, A.M.

EDITED BY

CHARLES GEORGE HERBERMANN, Ph.D

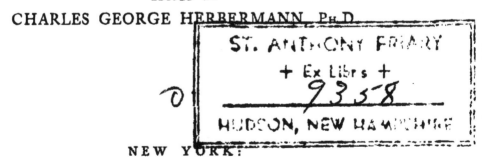

NEW YORK:

PUBLISHED BY
THE UNITED STATES CATHOLIC
HISTORICAL SOCIETY
1910

PREFACE

To Rev. Matthew Russell, S.J., and Rev. John J. Wynne, S.J., the Editor wishes in the first place to express his gratitude for placing at the disposal of the United States Catholic Historical Society the interesting diary of Lord Russell of Killowen, written during his visit to our country in 1883. It is always interesting and instructive "to see ourselves as others see us," and Lord Russell was a man of such sound judgment, good taste, keen observation, and catholic sympathies that his views on what he saw in the United States cannot fail to be instructive. Withal, the diary affords to the reader a vivid picture of family life and affection which cannot fail to charm every sympathetic heart.

The thanks of the Society are also due to the New York Bar Association for the photograph of Lord Russell's bust which graces its library, as well as to the management of the Northern Pacific Railroad for our illustrations of some of the leading incidents connected with Lord Russell's journey across our continent. Lastly, we express our thanks to the Hon. John P. Mitchel for his kindness in permitting us to reproduce the portrait of his distinguished grandfather.

Introduction

LORD RUSSELL of Killowen, Chief Justice of England, had always warm American sympathies. Far on in his career, when he was anything but a disappointed man, he told me that, if he had to start life again, he would be inclined to cast his lot under the Stars and Stripes.

He paid two visits to the United States. The first was during the Long Vacation of 1883; and it is of this visit that some account is given in the following pages. The second visit was in the autumn of 1896, when he was invited to deliver the annual address before the American Bar Association at Saratoga Springs. On this latter occasion he kept no diary, for he was accompanied by his wife, his daughter Lilian (now Mrs. Henry Drummond), and his son, the Hon. Charles Russell. He was also accompanied by his genial and gifted friend, Sir Frank Lockwood.

The first time he crossed the Atlantic, he was not Lord Russell nor even Sir Charles Russell, nor was he the principal figure of the party. He accompanied Lord Coleridge, whom he was to succeed as Chief Justice of England, and Sir James Hannen, whom, three years later, he was to address as Head of the Parnell Commission in a speech eight days long. Those things, and other things that happened afterwards, would have seemed improbable enough when Charles Stewart Parnell gave Charles Russell, Q. C., the day before he sailed from Liverpool, this letter of introduction to Justice Shea, New York:

HOUSE OF COMMONS, AUG. 13, 1883.
MY DEAR SIR:

Permit me to introduce to you Mr. Russell, who is visiting America. He is anxious to learn the status, political and social, and the views of our leading and representative countrymen in the States; and, although not a member of our party, he has always done what he could, both in and out of Parliament, from his own point of view, to serve the interests of Ireland. Need I say how much pleased I shall be if you can do anything to further the objects of his visit?

I am, my dear Sir,
Yours very truly,
CHAS. S. PARNELL.

The President of the Society which is publishing this diary will perhaps allow me to give this extract from his letter to Father John J. Wynne, S.J., who had placed it in his hands:

"I have read through Lord Russell's diary with considerable interest. It impresses me greatly as a portrait of a good affectionate father of a family interested in the education of his children. It reminded me of the great Villard glorification, in which General W.—— also took part. The diary is also a sad,

sympathetic memorial to the Indians and affords a
glimpse of the rising Pacific States in their infancy.
These features, together with Lord Russell's estimate
of the oratorical powers of Evarts and other Americans, some of which are quite instructive, I think
make the diary well worth publishing."

I will only add that it seems to me highly characteristic of my brother that amidst all the fatigue and
worries of such a journey he should have persevered
in jotting down his impressions in pencil, copy-book
after copy-book, and sending them week by week to
the dear ones at home, without the faintest notion of
such a fate as has now after a quarter of a century
befallen these hurried notes of travel.

The "Martin" referred to, especially in the account of the visit to California, was Mr. Patrick Martin, an Irish barrister, Q.C., and at one time M. P. for
Kilkenny.   That visit to California was undertaken
for the purpose of seeing the "Kate" of the diary,
namely, Mother Baptist Russell of St. Mary's Hospital, San Francisco. She was the second of three sisters who all became Sisters of Mercy.   In her
twenty-fifth year she led out a band of nuns from
Kinsale in the south of Ireland to the Golden Gate,
which they entered on the very day that the dogma
of the Immaculate Conception of the Blessed Virgin
Mary was solemnly proclaimed as an article of Catholic faith.   After a very full life of great utility, she
died in the hospital which she had founded and had

maintained some forty years, St. Mary's, San Francisco, in August, 1898, exactly two years before her brother. May they rest in peace.

As we have said, Lord Russell always felt a warm admiration for the United States of America. The feelings entertained towards him, especially by the American Bar, were expressed by the Ambassador to England, Mr. Joseph Choate, on the occasion of the unveiling of Lord Russell's statue in the central hall of the Royal Courts of Justice, January 11, 1905. Of the £3,200 subscribed for the memorial £900 came from the United States. As the representative of that great country, Mr. Choate said that "he would never have, and never had had, a more grateful and agreeable duty than to declare his affection, esteem, and admiration for the great jurist and noble gentleman whose statue had just been unveiled. The name and personality of Sir Charles Russell had long been familiar to the profession and to all the people of the United States. At the time of his untimely death he was a universal favourite amongst all parties, creeds, and sections in that country. The career of every great English lawyer was watched with the keenest interest by every disciple of Blackstone and Storey wherever our common language was spoken, and when a man rose step by step by sheer force of character, talents, and ambition, without the aid of patronage or influence, from the lowest rung of the ladder to the exalted position of Lord Chief Justice of England, he necessarily commanded their universal applause and admiration. There was no royal road to eminence at the Bar. It came by merit or it did not come at all; hence merit was sure to be widely appreciated wherever it was manifested. To the casual observer it was marvellous how from the moment he attained the ermine Lord Russell laid down all the contentions of advocacy and assumed the cold neutrality of an impartial judge. With whole-souled devotion he gave himself to the duties of his great office. To do justice was his only object; to ascertain the truth his only ambition. In his death the cause of truth, justice, and honour lost one of its noblest champions. In the proud position that he occupied so long as the greatest advocate of his time the world over, Sir Charles was an inspiring influence to his brethren everywhere, and as a supreme master of the dangerous art of cross-examination, so fatal when in feeble hands, so triumphant for truth when happily conducted, he was not only a peer in his own time, but his superior could not be found in all the annals of forensic history. He could elicit the truth from the most hopeless material, and could utterly destroy a false witness, for whom there was no escape from his searching and relentless pursuit. But he was much more and much nearer to them than the inspiring professional teacher and example. He made two prolonged visits to America, one in 1883 and the

other in 1896, both of which were ever-memorable,
for they brought him into close contact with the leading professional men, and his personal charm and
magnetism had full play.   Sir Charles was a strong
believer in personal intercourse between the responsi-
ble men of both countries as the best means of pro-
moting international harmony.   In every city that he
visited, in public and in private, he preached the gos-
pel of peace and goodwill between England and
America, and his constant efforts in that direction had
a powerful and enduring effect.   Just before his last
visit to America he had been leading counsel for
Great Britain before the Court of Arbitration which
disposed of the long vexed Behring Sea question,
and he conducted his case with such perfect fairness
and consummate ability that the triumph he won for
his country left no sting behind, but his opponents
from that day were counted amongst his life-long
friends and devoted admirers.   His last words to
them were still freshly remembered, and had had an
enduring influence for good: 'Who can doubt the influence that Great Britain and America possess for
ensuring the healthy progress and the peace of man-
kind?   But if this influence is to be fully felt they
must work together in cordial friendship, each people in its own sphere of action.   If they have great
power, they have also great responsibility.   No cause
they espouse can fail, no cause they oppose can triumph.   The future is in large part theirs.   They

have the making of history in the times that are to come. The greatest calamity that could befall would be strife that should divide them.' In season and out of season, at home and abroad, he preached the same doctrine, and it was not too much to say that no man had done more by wise counsel and earnest pleading to bring about the present happy relations between our two great countries than Lord Russell of Killowen. Who would wonder, then, that this memorial had been established to testify to future generations all his merits and virtues? On behalf of the judges and lawyers of America, and of all his countrymen, he blessed the name and memory of Lord Russell today. Might this statue, standing in the Temple of Justice which he so nobly adorned, show the lawyers of all time and of all nations what manner of man he was."

During the first of the two visits to the United States referred to above, Charles Russell sent home each week an account of his travels and experiences. It was characteristic of him to find time and energy to carry this out through his whole trip, though it must often have been exceedingly difficult. He jotted down in pencil notes of each day's doings and sent them home in batches according as opportunities occurred. These were transcribed very legibly into *cahiers* by no mercenary hand, but by his wife, who was able to decipher characters scrawled in the most untoward circumstances. And then, while the precious original was kept safe at home, the copy cir-culated among the scattered members of the family, one of whom *did* employ a mercenary hand to make a transcript which he now proposes to put partly into print.

MATTHEW RUSSELL, S.J.

L ORD RUSSELL of Killowen died on August 6, 1900. On the last day of that month, at the annual meeting of the American Bar Association held at Saratoga Springs, New York, Professor Bradley Thayer of Massachusetts moved the adoption of the following minutes:

"The American Bar Association has heard with peculiar sorrow of the death of Lord Russell of Killowen, Lord Chief Justice of England, and desires to enter upon its records some permanent expression of honour and esteem for his memory. The members of this Association had followed and known well that brilliant career which made Sir Charles Russell the conspicuous and admired leader of the English Bar, and they had rejoiced at the elevation of one so competent to the great office which he held with such distinction at the time of his death. Four years ago we welcomed him here as our chief guest. Recalling now the noble address which he delivered to us on the 30th of August, 1896, and the deep-felt enthusiasm inspired in the hearts of all who listened to him, the members of this Association desire to express their admiration for the manner in which he filled his high office, their grateful recollection of his visit here, their affectionate regard for his memory, and their respectful sympathy with the Bench and Bar of England in so great a loss to our common profession."

NOTES OF A TRIP TO THE UNITED STATES

In the Summer of 1883

BY CHARLES RUSSELL, Q.C.

TUESDAY, AUGUST 14, 1883.

EMBARKED by special tender at 1.30 with Arthur, Mr. Clark, and Darling and my good old friend John Yates who came to see me off. Arthur and Mr. Clark had got free passes to Queenstown. Sailed about 5.30.

Weather tolerable. Some wind and rain, and at times a roughish sea.

Lord Chief Justice Coleridge and his son Herbert, Sir James Hannen and his son (at the Bar) and P. Martin, Q.C., M.P. for Kilkenny, formed what I call my party, all very cheery and jolly; the Lord Chief Justice apparently inexhaustible in story.

Reached Queenstown at 11.30 A.M. Wednesday, August 15, 1883. Our party went ashore in a tender, where Arthur and Mr. Clark left us.

We went in a body to the Cathedral and heard High Mass. A large congregation in a noble building. The music (Mozart No. 3, I think) very poorly rendered, the celebrant's singing awful. No ear and less voice. Architect of church, Pugin. The Lord

Chief Justice told me Hannen was greatly impressed, and that the latter told him that, if he could believe, he would be a Catholic. By the way, Hannen told me his grandfather was a Catholic and a Cork man. He said his father was "caught" (whatever that means) early and brought up a Protestant. He added he would like to explore Cork and find out, if he could, the hovel in which his forefathers lived. All the same I think he would be better pleased *not* to find out "the hovel."

The harbour of Queenstown and the town looked remarkably well. The weather was good; it was a holiday (the Assumption) and there was a regatta on.

At five o'clock we got back to our ship and were underway at about 5.20 P.M., and by 10 o'clock we had well cleared the Fastnetts (Lighthouse) and had lost sight of Ireland.

The weather was roughish, and when we got clear of the shelter of the Irish Coast (the wind was blowing from the northwest) it was very ugly. At 2 A.M. on Thursday I was "overcome," but since then have been pretty well, though feeling still shaky. I hated, cordially hated up to yesterday evening, several unfeeling brutes, who go stamping about in the rudest health, laughing and smoking and suffering nothing apparently! However, since I have begun to feel better myself, I look with less ferocity on their unfeeling behaviour.

THURSDAY, AUGUST 16, 1883.

I FIND I've run into this day in my previous note. It (this day) was almost uneventful.

The weather was not the worst and was far from the best. We've had since we left Queenstown a continuous head-wind, i.e., from the west, and the sea considerably "tumbly." The Captain (Gleadell) objects much more to the latter than the former. A head-wind gives "go" to the furnaces by improving the draught in the engine-room and so enables them to get more out of the engines; but the tumble of the sea takes the propeller out of the water while the vessel pitches and so much power goes to waste. The great excitement of the day is an "Auction Pool" as to the ship's run for twenty-four hours, i.e., from 12 o'clock noon of to-day (Thursday) till 12 o'clock to-morrow (Friday). It is computed as likely that the run will not be much less than 235 miles nor more than 255 or thereabouts. The highest number includes all above it and the lowest all below it. These and the intermediate numbers are put up to auction, each bidder to start with paying a dollar for the right to bid. The numbers vary in price, No. 235 having brought nearly £5. I am writing this on Friday, before the actual run is ascertained, but it is thought the run will be about 237. The run itself is calculated by reference to the ship's latitude and longitude, which are in turn calculated by the aid of the sextant when the sun is plainly visible. Without the sun clearly visible they can do nothing.

FRIDAY, AUGUST 17, 1883.

WE'VE about 190 saloon passengers and altogether on board, including crew and steerage, a little under a thousand souls. The arrangements are wonderfully good, both in steerage and saloon parts. In the former the people supply their own bedding, and many have hardly any; but as to food they are very well off apparently and often get their table supplemented by very substantial crumbs from their richer neighbours. I've got a stateroom all to myself and am very comfortable. I am not as steady as I should be on *terra firma*, but I feel that the worst is over and that even if the weather became fierce I should not wholly succumb. The run since 12 o'clock yesterday just announced as 319, which is considerably below popular expectation. In good weather and under highly favourable conditions the *Celtic* will do over 350 miles.

The order of events for the day is as follows:

Breakfast, from 9 to 10.30.

Porridge (which I've stuck to principally), tea, etc., and a great number of dishes of the ordinary English kind. The distinct and only American things which we so far noticed are fried oysters, corn cakes (made of Indian corn), green corn cooked and tomatoes.

Luncheon, from 1 P.M. to 2 o'clock.

Cold (but you can have hot) soups.

Dinner, 6 o'clock.

Very great variety of ordinary English dishes and I've not come across any distinctively American dishes. Ocasionally sauces which do not sound English, as huckleberry sauce, cranberry sauce served with goose and joints occasionally. There is a very good biscuit, too, called Boston crackers, which are excellent when rebaked in the oven and put upon the table piping hot.

As to the people, there seem very few at all interesting so far as I've yet seen.

There is a Mrs. Kidd and family by whom I've been rather taken. She is a kindly little body bent on looking after everybody who needs looking after. She has a charming little daughter, with whom I've nearly fallen in love. Arthur saw her, and I think admires her. There is a lot of doctors; one, a Dr. T——, told me his income was some $85,000, which, I should say, is a great deal more than any English doctor or surgeon makes. He seemed to be rather a "bounder," and he didn't speak over-generously of another M.D. in New York, Dr. Marion Simms, who (I afterwards learned) is a surgeon of very great repute.

SATURDAY, AUGUST 18, 1883.

THE great event to-day (for me) is the fact that I
won the Pool on the ship's run. The lowest No.
was 315, which carried with it all Nos. lower down.
At auction I bid three guineas for it and was declared
buyer. There were in the Pool some £18, so that I
won about £14.

The actual run was 304 miles, or 15 miles less
than in the prior 24 hours.

We are still meeting a stiffish head-wind, i.e., from
the west (called—I mention this for Charlie's information—"fresh breeze" in the log). The sea,
too, is lumpy, and altogether, if the weather does
not change, it is not improbable that we shall not see
the end of our voyage before this day-week, i.e., Saturday the 25th instant.

It is a very striking fact, as illustrated by the immensity of the track we are travelling along, that we
have only seen altogether three sails since we lost
sight of Ireland. Also a curious fact, that we find
ourselves attended by solitary seagulls who have to
go over 1,000 miles before they can get a resting-
place for their feet, and although we are travelling at
the rate of from twelve to thirteen knots an hour
these birds are able, apparently without an effort and
against a head-wind, to keep pace with us.

So far I rather share Oscar Wilde's ideas on the
subject of the Atlantic. I am disappointed, but I

must add agreeably disappointed in one sense. Thus:
The waves are certainly not at all as grand or striking as I thought they would be; but on the other
hand the absence of this grandeur makes the actual
voyage comfortable. I do not mean to say that I
feel as comfortable as on land, but I am no longer
squeamish and I move about in at least comparative
comfort. If on the other hand the Atlantic were to
assert its grandeur to the extent of washing our hurricane or promenade deck and so to require the se-
curing of all the passengers below, I need hardly say
that matters would be altered very much for the
worse.

SUNDAY, AUGUST 19, 1883.

MOST strange! I left off writing yesterday's Note
about 5 o'clock, and a little before six the wind
went to the south, increased in force and before
7 o'clock we had a fearful sea on, accompanied by a
wind which came in great gusts. At first the seamen
made light of the weather; but it is duly logged to-
day as "strong gales with violent squalls" which
Charlie will tell you is strong nautical language. The
Atlantic certainly did look very imposing. As far
as the horizon all round, the "white horses" running
wild and now and then the wind getting hold of the
tip of a wave scattered it in a shower over the length
of the ship. At times, too, the ship, which had just
mounted a small wave, met a big one before it had

time to gather itself together again and in it went— bows well down, deluging the decks to quite amidships. All the time, however, I failed to see any of the mast-head-high waves which one has heard about. The *Celtic* behaved well—with all the buoyancy of her race—and although the rolling was trying it was, on the whole, so regular and free from jerkiness that I for one managed to preserve my dignity.

The real unpleasantness was at night. All the ordinary ventilators, which in fine weather are open, were closed (all through which water as well as air might get) : the portlight's covers screwed down and all the passenger-approaches to the decks closed and secured. The noise was a fearful compound of sounds—the fall of water, the clanging of chains, the banging of doors, the creaking of the ship, the startling rumble of the steering-gear, and now and again the frightened cry of passengers. Notwithstanding all this I managed to sleep a little—very little—and I was heartily glad when morning came.

To-day is a dull day, for poker and other like games are forbidden. There was a kind of religious service this morning, at which, however, I did not assist.

The run to-day up to 12 noon from previous noon was only 286 as against 304 for the previous day.

It is curious to note the allowance made for difference of time. As we get west, an addition is made of about half an hour per day. Thus the last twenty-four hours were computed at twenty-four and a half hours. I've not altered my watch since we left England, and I am now about three hours or so in advance of the true time.

I had a long talk yesterday and to-day with an Albany man about American Government, local and general, and his view of it is far from flattering. He says corruption is everywhere, from the highest stratum to the lowest, and he vigorously denounces the caucus system, by which, as he says, the mass of uninstructed voters is made to vote almost mechanically in obedience to the will of the wire-pullers. This is very much what Conservatives in England say in denouncing Chamberlain and the Birmingham caucus. I shall no doubt hear the other side of the question before long. The same gentleman was eloquent about the lowering influence of the Irish vote in the cities. He says they are a great power, if not *the* great power in all the great cities—where for the purposes of local or general politics the franchise is possessed by all men of a certain length of residence —in other words, universal manhood suffrage. He says, with some justice apparently, that the vast majority of this class have no stake in the country and little knowledge of what is best for the country, and they are thus left a prey to the corrupt or expert wire-pullers who get hold of and use them for their own purposes. He points out that the Irish emigrants, who for the most part are recruited from the farming

class in Ireland, generally congregate in the towns
and do *not* take as kindly as German and other Con-
tinental emigrants to farming. He says there is practically no such thing as failure known amongst the
classes who have taken to farms. No doubt the vast
majority of the Irish stick to the towns because no arrangements have been made for taking them out
West and placing them on farms there, and they are
generally too poor and too ignorant to make the effort westward for themselves.

It is, I fear, too true that in the big towns our people are still the hewers of wood and drawers of water.
I wish they were no worse than this—but they also fill
the jails and are the heaviest drain on the poor-rate
funds! Of course all this is explicable without involving any *general* or grave reflection upon our people. Will the day ever come when these explanations
shall be no longer needed?

Run yesterday 304 miles: to-day 286.

MONDAY, AUGUST 20, 1883.

A MOST agreeable change! Since about 11 o'clock
yesterday the weather has taken up wonderfully.
The sea is as smooth as Carlingford Bay in ordinary
weather, and barring a Scotch mist now and then a
seat on the hurricane deck is everything desirable.

The ship's company is just now engaged in getting
up a concert—amateur—for the benefit of the Sea-

men's Hospital, Liverpool. The Lord Chief Justice is to preside. It is funny to note the difference in the attendance at meals which a change to kindly weather makes. In the bad weather few ladies and comparatively few gentlemen appear, but to-day all hands turn up and the ladies seem to be beginning to take a recovered pride in their dress and general personal appearance. There are several young ladies who are certainly entitled to rank as good looking, but there are no beauties!

There is, as I write (11.55) great excitement about the run. This is the first fair day's weather for steaming. The betting is for between 330 miles and 340 miles in the twenty-four hours or rather in the twenty-four and a half hours.

P. S. Run 337 miles.

TUESDAY, AUGUST 21, 1883.

THIS day-week we sailed from the Mersey! This day-week, do you say? Why, it seems a month since, at the least. It is a matter for scientific observation that, when the events happening around you or in which you are taking part are novel, you fail to take correct note of time; and while in fact it passes quickly and unobserved from hour to hour, you exaggerate it as you look back upon what has happened. Certainly it seems very long since Arthur left in the tender. To-day the beautiful weather continues, but it is warmer, balmier than heretofore, which tells the instructed amongst us that we are under the softening, not to say, melting influence of the Gulf Stream.

[Explain what the Gulf Stream is, Eily, to your younger brother and sisters!]

The salt-water bath this morning was perfectly delicious. You open a plug and in comes rolling the pure blue Atlantic water! I revelled in it.

Everything went well to-day. Our run the best so far, i.e., 348 miles as against 337 yesterday.

We are all looking forward in expectancy to the concert this evening; but this will come into to-morrow's (Wednesday's) Note. It is rumoured there is a brilliant public singer amongst us, but apparently no one is certain about it. The Lord Chief Justice is to preside, and, as announced in the Bills, carriages are ordered for 10.30.

Not the least pleasurable part of the fine-weather-results is its effect on the steerage passengers. Bad weather for them means unmitigated discomfort, but when, as for the past two days, the sea is calm and the weather genial, they crowd the 'tween decks, babies and all, and seem thoroughly to enjoy their surroundings.

There are few Irish amongst them, and none of them present the appearance of abject poverty. They are fairly well clad and have not that emaciated look which one has too often seen in Ireland and in the

JOHN DUKE LORD COLERIDGE,
LORD CHIEF JUSTICE OF ENGLAND

big towns in England sometimes—and which is commonly caused by stint of good food.

THE concert went off remarkably well. The music selected was all very good, and a considerable part of it was very well rendered. I was amongst the performers, if you please! They insisted on my giving my name as a decoy for others, but with the solemn assurance that I was *not* to be called into active service. They broke faith with me, however, and I gave them (to vary the musical monotony) a short recitation, which was received with great applause. I will let you all guess what it was: it was short, it was blank verse, and it was *not* serious.

An old New York doctor (Marion Simms) read an account of some incidents of the War of Independence—more or less interesting—and lugged in a kind of congratulatory address to the Lord Chief Justice, who responded in his *suaviter-in-modo* best style. (Bertie, translate this for your sisters.) On the whole, the evening was very enjoyable, and we got up a collection of £25 for the Seamen's Orphans' Home, Liverpool. I should before have said that one of the most effective features of the musical part of the entertainment was a "Smoke Room" chorus in which the only distinguishable sentiment was that it was "easy to roll a man down"; but as the air was

"Coming thro' the Rye" it afforded a good opportunity to all so minded to join in the general clamour.

This morning (Wednesday) I got up at 4.30 to see the sun rise from the bosom of the Atlantic; and certainly the view from the "Whale's back" (a covered part forward) all round was very striking. All round, the horizon sharply definable and free from fog—nothing to be seen but water—water everywhere! No sail, no birds, no porpoises, nothing. The sunrise itself could not compare in beauty and richness of colour with some I've seen from the Connemara coast. Oddly enough I've not seen any sunset. The weather has at sunset been invariably so foggy that nothing could be made of it.

THURSDAY, AUGUST 23, 1883.

OUR run yesterday as recorded was only 246 miles, although the conditions generally seemed uncommonly favourable. I say *as recorded*, because there is an acknowledged source of error in the mode of reckoning. Thus: The reckoning is accurately to be made at noon each day, but then only when there is no fog to prevent the line of the horizon being clearly seen. Then what is called an "observation" is taken, by which the position of the ship is definitely fixed; but if no such observation can be taken because of fog or of the sun being obscured by clouds, then the ship's position is got at by "dead reckoning," which, as I understand it, means starting from the last ascertained position, computing approximately the distance traversed, taking into account speed of engines, forces of wind, tide, etc., whether for or against.

An observation can also be made from the stars, but the operation is a more delicate one and not so reliable; therefore in all cases it follows that, if for (say) two days no observation has been obtained, the "dead reckoning" computation may be out considerably; and when on the third day accurate observation is made, which shows the distance traversed in the interval from the previous observation, the balance only of that distance, *after* deducting the recorded distances to the two preceding days, is given as the run of the third day. It is clear, therefore, that the third day's record may be much less than or greater than the actual distance traversed on that day.

Nothing could exceed the charm of the past three days. The weather has been everything that could be desired: the sun shining brilliantly; the seas almost smooth, and a pleasant light wind tempering what would otherwise have been oppressive heat.

Even now within 300 miles of Sandy Hook (look at your map, Eily) we see but few sailing vessels or steamships, but the porpoises and flying-fish are playing about us, and men, women, and children are all on deck, and full of fun and frolic—every one in good spirits.

Last night's was the last Pool on the run, for we hope to be in New York for breakfast to-morrow (Friday morning); and now the Pool is the Pilot Pool. This means that there being (say) twenty-six Pilot-boats, all numbered from 1 upwards, the winner of the Pool is he who will draw the No. of the boat which contains our pilot. My boats are numbered 16 and 22, and I am not gratified to learn that one of them is supposed to be at the bottom of the sea at this moment.

Last night we had a grand sunset. The horizon was hazy, and as usual exaggerated the size of the sun, which, sinking in great splendour and dignity, recalled vividly

"The Monarch Day has flung his crown of gold
    And fiery mantle down into the River."[1]

This morning I was called at 5 o'clock, and for the first time saw the sun rising from the bosom of this great ocean. It was truly a grand sight! The Captain allowed me to go up to the "crow's nest" (a high lookout point forward). It is impossible to convey the striking beauty of the scene. The sea smooth literally as a mirror. The sky was a cold greyish-blue save where in the east the glow of the coming sun crimsoned or began to crimson the horizon—

"The Morn in rosy mantle clad."

All round the horizon, which in unbroken circle

[1] Rosa Mulholland's "Irene," in *The Cornhill Magazine*. Reprinted in her volume, "Vagrant Verses."

surrounds you—nothing, nothing to be seen but the
great waste of waters except the striking brilliant
pageant in the east, heralding the approach of the
new Monarch, Day. In fewer moments than it takes
to write these lines the sun has begun to appear above
the sharp line of the horizon, apparently twice its
normal size, and clothed in rich deep crimson, and in
another short space it has raised itself from the
waters; and before your eye is satisfied with dwelling
upon its beauty, it begins imperiously to assert itself,
and you dare no longer look it in the face. There
are faiths for which there is less to be said than for
that of the worshippers of the sun. I think reverential
awe would, in some sort, be present to most minds in
view of this morning's glorious sunrise. It must have
been at such a time as this that the founder of the
Sun-faith received his revelation.

FRIDAY, AUGUST 24, 1883.

NEW YORK! Brunswick Hotel. Arrived! I must
first go back a little. We were due at Sandy
Hook about 5 o'clock this morning, and so there were
many who did not care to seek their berths at all.
The weather was delicious. The moon and stars
shining upon an apparently motionless sea. There
were sounds of gaiety in all directions—songs, danc-
ing, practical jokes, and so forth. The betting, too,
was fast and furious, and the events wagered upon

ludicrous in the extreme; for instance, we were hourly
expecting to meet our Pilot, and many were the wagers as to his age, whether married or single, whether
he wore a moustache, whether the years of his age
were odd or even, and, as a climax of absurdity,
one of the most exciting events was whether in
boarding our ship his left or his right foot first
touched the deck! I will not stop to recount the
various issues of those wagers, except to say the
last-named event was undecided, as he jumped on
deck!

About 5 o'clock I first sighted America—that is,
Sandy Hook, and presently before the rising sun the
clouds "vamoosed"[1] and showed us Long Island on
our right or starboard hand, and Staten Island on our
left or port hand. (Eily, recur to your map.) About
8 or 10 miles from New York our ship stopped for
the Quarantine examination, and here were in waiting two steamboats for two very different parties on
board ship. One of these was crowded with the
local friends of two New York celebrities, Jim Al-
leger [name illegible] and Will Simpson, who came
out to welcome the latter home, their boat being gaily
decorated with all manner of flags. Each of the
party on board was furnished with a kind of fog-
horn which at intervals was fiercely blown and produced the most discordant sounds—which, however,

[1]This is United States slang for "disappeared quickly," from
the Spanish *vamos,* "let us go."

seemed greatly to gratify the parties immediately concerned.

The other boat was for the Lord Chief Justice and party and was the very beautiful steam-yacht of Mr. Gerry, a member of the New York Bar, and one of the Reception Committee.

Into this we got, and in this we steamed into the very noble harbour of New York. The map will show sufficiently the conformation and the relative positions of New York, with Brooklyn on the right (as we steamed up) and Jersey City on the left. The happy idea of our friends (and it was *indeed* a happy idea) was to give us a kind of *coup d'œil* of the three cities.

I say at once I had no idea of the beauty and the grandeur of the place. Two main impressions were forced upon me—one that the atmosphere had a transparent clearness which even in Southern France I had never seen equalled, and the other that, as befits a mighty Continent, things were (except the mere aggregation of houses) on a much grander scale than in our little islands.

We steamed up between Long Island (Brooklyn) and New York under the famous Suspension Bridge which connects the two cities together. In space and lightness of appearance (elegance one might say) it greatly exceeds anything of the kind I ever saw. Compared with our hideous railway bridges over the Thames, it is a thing of beauty. It was about 160

feet above our heads and on it are *two* railroads,
two carriage roads and a footway about 25 feet
wide!

On each side of the river is the vast shipping of
New York *in the open river,* but so well protected all
round from tempest as to render docks such as we
have in Liverpool and London wholly unnecessary.
Protection from tempest, however, would not be
enough to render docks unnecessary which in London,
Liverpool, and so forth are necessary in order to secure therein sufficient depths of water. But in New
York the tide rises and falls only about 6 feet (as
against 16 to 30 feet in London and Liverpool), and
there is ample depth for the shipping at all states of
the tide along the riverside wharves.

We steamed up the river and to the New York
side of two islands on which are built the principal
City institutions of the jail, reformatory, etc., character. The principal island is called Blackwell's. The
banks on either side, as we sailed up, are picturesque; and here and there are to be seen traces of
what were formerly country-house residences, but
which have been pushed out further by aggressive city
industries.

One melancholy spot—melancholy and indeed
humiliating to an Irishman and to those who are ac-
countable for the government of Ireland—was
pointed out. Just outside the city and on a waste
desolate spot on the river bank are a number of

wooden shanties—wretched structures and affording but scant protection from wind and rain. You will guess what they are? They are the abodes now, as they for years have been, of Irish squatters—poor creatures who, landed here moneyless and friendless, were fain to put up with shelter which a well-bred dog would scorn. These erections are of course trespasses carelessly suffered, or it may be good-naturedly permitted by the owner of the ground so long as he has no present use for it; *but* when he has, out go the miserable inmates neck and crop by summary process The jails and reformatory system here contemplates the productive labour of the inmates as an important self-supporting factor. Query. Why not in Great Britain and Ireland? Query. Mackonachie's reformatory system?

Still steaming up, we get into the Long Island Sound, putting about stern down the river again—this time on the Brooklyn side of the river and Blackwell's Island.

Then began our first American meal, and a very good beginning it was. Under an awning which sheltered us from the fierce heat, and at the same time made the most of the cooling breeze, we had a breakfast of a very excellent kind and distinctly Parisian in its main features with a dash of Americanism—the latter principally in the shape of a champagne cocktail which prefaced the entertainment. Fish cutlets. omelette, salad, melons, other fruit, backed up by delicious hot corn-cakes, claret, champagne, and coffee, made up our bill of fare.

Before breakfast was over, we had again passed under the Brooklyn Suspension Bridge and were passing close by a spot full of sad and bitter memories (I fear) to many people, but also full of hopefulness to many more, I believe. I mean Castle Garden, New York, where all the emigrants are usually landed. What has already become of those landed to-day? Some no doubt have had their destination fixed, but many, I believe, have come out, hoping for something to turn up and not knowing where to look for that something.

Anyway, New York has swallowed them up and they have disappeared, making no sign.

Still we continue steaming down the river, and now we have reached the point where the Hudson River runs to the north, round the north and west of New York. This river is called the Rhine of America, and up to West Point, on the way to Albany (which is the capital of the State of New York), is said to be extremely beautiful. I propose judging for myself one of these days. Finally we land at a wharf near Twentieth St., where two carriages await us. Sir J. Hannen and son, Martin and myself are deposited at the Brunswick, and the Lord Chief Justice is taken on to the private residence of Colonel Shepard, Barrister, who is the chairman of the Entertaining Committee.

I think, but I am not sure, that we are considered to be guests here.

I am greatly charmed by what I have seen, but physically I feel thoroughly done up, and as I've been up since 4 o'clock this morning nothing would be half so agreeable to me as a bath and a good sleep. But the latter is not yet attainable. To-night we have a serious dinner engagement at which we are to meet the city magnates; but to-morrow we propose loafing about leisurely on our own account. I feel wonderfully well and believe the voyage has done me a world of good. Tell Bertie I've not yet got my land legs. The floors have just yet a very awkward and perplexing habit of rising up to meet you, and you keep balancing yourself sailor-like as if still on the deck of the good ship—and good ship she is—the *Celtic*.

SATURDAY, AUGUST 25, 1883.

FRIDAY afternoon was spent almost as agreeably as the forenoon. Mr. Holmes, Attorney-Barrister and Counsel for the Northern Pacific Railroad Company, insisted on bringing our party to lunch at the Union League Club, Fifth Avenue, and after a very appetising meal there, we were driven round and through and up and down the Central Park, which seems to be of great size and beautifully laid out, covered with striking statues of Columbian big men, and planted with a wondrous variety of tree, shrub, and flower, which nevertheless all come from this great continent.

The club-life is an important element in society here, and we have been temporarily made members of the three principal ones in New York: the Union, the Union League, and the Knickerbocker. Their interior arrangements as to furniture and disposition of space are far superior to anything in England; and their adoption of the elevator enables them to have magnificent and very useful rooms high-up—higher than our highest club-houses. If one must be critical, perhaps those I have seen are in some respects a trifle "loud," according to English notions. At 7.30 we dined, to meet the Lord Chief at Mr. Shepard's house, which, as becomes the son-in-law of the mighty Vanderbilt, is grand, and luxuriantly furnished. There are three Vanderbilt houses together, that is, that of *the* Vanderbilt and those of two of his sons-in-law; and they are so arranged that, while normally wholly independent of one another, they are capable, on great receptions, of being all thrown into one, when the effect may be guessed.

At dinner each guest was asked to put his autograph on his own and every other guest's menu. I enclose mine. I have appended a note of the titles of those of the guests I learned about.

Mrs. Shepard appeared a reasonably intelligent and good-looking lady (for an heiress) and was free from all airs. She only appeared before dinner, as it was what the Americans call a "Stag" dinner.

Mr. Sullivan (himself obviously of Irish descent) remarked we were a good typical representative party of Englishmen. I staggered the party by telling them that of the six, only the Lord Chief and his son were English, for that Sir James Hannen was only an Irishman once removed, and that Martin and I were Irish down to our toe-nails.

The dinner was good—the company I thought no way brilliant in conversation; but it is fair to remember that formal dinners are not the best places to make the most of any man's humour. I went to bed thoroughly tired; my bed rocking a little; and I slept the sleep which "knits up the ravelled sleave of care," for I awoke at 7 o'clock to a bright clear morning, refreshed and cheerful.

SUNDAY, AUGUST 26, 1883.

ON Saturday night Martin received through me (I was already an invited guest) an invitation to an excursion under the auspices and at the charge of Henry Villard, President of the Northern Pacific Railroad Company. It is in connection with the opening by them of a new line right through from St. Paul (see map) to Portland on the Pacific. We are in advance of the main body, which we are to join at St. Paul, d. v., next Monday. It will probably save us a good many pounds in railway tickets and will be pleasant withal.

Martin and I will probably leave the excursion party at Portland, and, if possible, find our way back by San Francisco and the Southern Union Pacific— probably by St. Louis, Cincinnati, Philadelphia, and New York.

The Cathedral Church of Saint Patrick, Fifth Avenue, is *the* church of New York, as far as architectural beauty and grandeur are concerned. It is a very grand building indeed, not unlike the Dundalk Church, but on a much grander scale, and with two spires or towers still incomplete, and for which it is computed £50,000 sterling will be needed. It is made of a stone which is called here marble, but which seems to me very like our granite but much whiter, having much less mica in it. The principal Protestant Church is Episcopal. Low: it is called Trinity Church, and is remarkable in this—that every stone of it was imported from England! This is not an exceptional case, it seems; indeed a Pennsylvania gentleman informed us that it was the case with many of the older churches in that State. Martin and I were both struck by the smallness of the Catholic congregation. The church was not half filled. True, it was High Mass and this is the dull season, but still we thought it remarkable. At 6.30 P.M. we crossed to Jersey City, which is divided from New York by the Hudson River; and by the Erie Railway we left for Niagara *via* Buffalo, arriving at the Falls about 7 A.M.

The night in the Pullman Car and breakfast in the morning (I know you will be surprised, Madam) were not at all disagreeable. The country *en route* is in many places extremely picturesque; and a fair sprinkling of population, with here and there a biggish town, are to be found all along the line. Still the cultivation is of the scratchy-patchy order; the regular fencing of fields only seen at intervals, and, compared with the appearance of England, Ireland, and Scotland, the whole thing looks raw, unkempt, and wild.

I may say here, by the way, that the *only* thing in which towns and country here are (so far as I have noticed) inferior to the old country, is the matter of roads and streets. These are very bad in New York, and *nowhere* along the line of railway have I noticed any regularly made roads, although there seems to be wisely reserved everywhere, in town and country, *ample space* for street and road accommodation.

At Niagara the day was broiling, and our first care was to engage a carriage (at an exorbitant price). With water enough to turn the world's machinery, the local authorities had not utilized a drop to lay the roads, inches thick in dust.

What shall I say about Niagara? Well, to begin with, for the first time I find the description given of this remarkable spot fairly do it justice as far as description can.   Its wonderful beauty and grandeur must be seen to be appreciated.

The vast waters of lakes Michigan, Huron, and Erie lend their mighty forces to send the water on its way by Lake Ontario to the St. Lawrence River, with terrific pressure through the narrow channel formed in rock which connects Lake Erie with Lake Ontario and which is called Niagara River.   A short way above the Falls the rush of the waters is divided by a small island called Goat Island.   The fall to the east of this island is called the American Fall, that to the west the Canadian; the latter is by far the grander in every way, depth of fall, volume of water, etc. Above the fall the effect is most striking.   The great mass of boiling, angry water tears furiously along and seems suddenly to drop into the bowels of the earth and disappear—so sheer and sudden is the fall—and the roar of the fallen and falling waters is all that is noticeable.   Below the fall the effect is remarkable and startling.   Notwithstanding the enormous volume of water and the height of its fall, it is literally true, that within a few yards of the Fall the surface of the water is perfectly clear and almost quiescent! Fancy this, and after a fall of some 160 feet over the sheer cliff!   In fact, the depth of the river is about another 160 feet, and it would appear that the descending water hides its fury under the calm surface-water and only reappears some two miles lower down the river. In other words, there is a strong under-surface current which comes to sight again about the spot where the Rapids begin, in which the ill-fated Captain Webb lately met his death. These rapids are simply parts of the river where the channel is rather contracted, and the fall in the river bed considerable, so that there is not only a rapid but a troubled, broken rush of the waters. It is surmised that in the course are rocks and that Captain Webb, partly sucked down by one of the under-currents which prevail, was violently carried against some of them. It appears a small steamship successfully ran the rapids, and on the American side, they are already building another for the like purpose. The exactions and the mode of exactions at Niagara are intolerable. A squint at Nature anywhere here costs you from fifty cents to a dollar. It is not creditable to the two governments to allow this state of things.

In the evening we left for Chicago *via* the Grand Trunk Railway, through Port Huron, which is on Lake Huron, and we arrived at 9 A.M. at Chicago. The population along the line, *en route,* seemed rather thicker than on the Sunday's journey, and the land better tilled; but this would be no safe indication of the state of things farther away from the line.

I am greatly exercised in my mind as to the trees in the United States and in Canada. I have, as yet, seen no finer timber—for instance, none at all equalling what is to be seen in any English demesne. But

more: the trees have not the look of age the English
trees have. It cannot be that the existing trees are
the result of a new and recent planting. I shall get
some one to answer my doubts for me. So far, I
have not been able to exclaim with any confidence—
"This is the forest primeval."[1]   On all sides are to
be seen signs of vigorous and recent clearance—
what is called lumber clearance by the natives. The
houses almost invariably in the country places and
frequently in the towns are made of wood; but nowhere have I seen any sign of want—on the contrary,
there are visible everywhere satisfactory indications
of rough plenty and progress.

At the country stations (called here depots) I've
come across a good many Irishmen and Scotchmen,
but comparatively few Englishmen. Generally, with
all, the expression is one of satisfaction and content
with their condition, but occasionally an Irishman
will tell you that living is very dear and that he could
live just as well at home. I've not yet seen any Irish
Land Settlement, and I am very doubtful whether I
shall. I intend to try.

TUESDAY, AUGUST 28, 1883.

ARRIVED at 9 o'clock at Chicago, Grand Pacific
Hotel.

This is certainly a very remarkable but not at all
interesting city. Its staple businesses are grain-stor-

[1]The first words of Longfellow's "Evangeline"

ing, pig-killing, meat-preserving, etc., etc. These are useful trades, but not soul-inspiring. All the same, there are some remarkable points in the history of the place. The city is not more than fifty years old. Originally it was entirely built of wood, but in 1871 a fearful fire reduced two-thirds or more of the town to ashes. Since '71 it has not only been rebuilt in stone with noble buildings and fine streets— even wider than those of New York—but it has more than trebled its population, until now, with a population approaching three-quarters of a million, it is about second in population and certainly second in trade of all the cities of the States. Its hotels are enormous and with all possible modern comforts and improvements. The Palace House is said to be the largest hotel in the world.

Still with all this it is far from being a graceful or even a cleanly city. The streets are certainly wide, but they are shockingly paved, and they are spoiled by numerous tramways: again the streets are not in all cases continuously and regularly built upon, and, out of the principal thoroughfares, there is a raw, unfinished, generally unkempt appearance, which recalls the early description of American cities by Dickens. In one respect the city authorities pre-eminently deserve credit. They have secured for the Chicago of the future and the present the most extensive parks to be found in connection with any American city, or probably any city in the world. They have in the parks and along the Lake (Michigan) on which the city abuts, secured for the public for all time, some 35 miles of drives through well-wooded and well-arranged parklands. The lake (pray understand, May!) is about as big as England and Scotland put together, and makes Chicago, to all intents and all appearance, a seaport. In the offing you see big three-masted vessels, and there is a large quay or pier along and opposite the entrance of the River Chicago, which river floats vessels of large tonnage right into the heart of the city.

I made the acquaintance of two local celebrities (Irish), namely Paddy Ryan and Michael McDonald. Paddy may be dismissed with the statement that he is a fighting-man lately defeated in the twenty-four-foot ring by a compatriot, Sullivan. He is a Tipperary man. He left Ireland at eight years of age. He now keeps a liquor store and seems a good-natured lumbering chap of about six feet high and weighs about seventeen stone. Michael McDonald deserves more than a passing word. He, too, keeps a liquor store, a gambling house (in spite of the authorities), and he "runs" a granite quarry. But his principal importance arises from his political position. He is supposed to direct and control what is called the rowdy element in Chicago—largely made up of our countrymen—and this gives him very great local influence. He is a rough diamond, not over-scrupulous, with a decisive, masterful way about him, which clearly marks him out as a leader of men. He shows great knowledge of European politics, or at least of those of France and Great Britain. He is keenly Irish, but was loud in his condemnation of the assassination and dynamite policy. His friends claim for him that he returned the present Mayor of Chicago —the first Democratic mayor returned for Chicago for thirty years.

By far the most interesting feature of our stay in Chicago, however, was a visit to Pullman, a small town about sixteen miles from Chicago and called after the inventor of the travelling and sleeping car, which is also called after him. No one who has not had to travel long distances, and by night, can fully appreciate the boon to many, many thousands which the Pullman car really is. Since last Sunday (I am writing on Wednesday) we have travelled about 1,200 miles and spent two nights in the Pullman, and I affirm I do not feel now as tired as I have frequently done travelling from London to Liverpool. It is difficult to say where the difference (I know you dislike sleeping cars) in favour of the system exists, but it does and markedly. You can move about, go out now and then to end of car, in the open air, easily alight at each depot, occasionally vary the monotony by comfortably washing your hands and brushing your hair (if you have any) and, when nature calls out for sustenance, you are served with what you need in a cleanly, comfortable way in your carriage. And finally when night has closed in upon you, you can go to bed, really to bed, and with a sense of refreshment and relief. I have said nothing about a point which, however, greatly concerns the comfort of the journey, I mean the fact that the attendant is unceasing in his perambulation up and down, and down and up the train, with papers, books, cards, fruit, bon-bons, etc. The nature of the contract and relation of the Pullman Company to and with the Railway Company which runs their cars is remarkable. The Pullman Company lets the cars to the Railway Company, and the former undertakes to keep it in repair for three cents per mile traversed, and it also supplies a conductor and a porter or attendant for each car. The Pullman Company then receives all that is paid for the use of their car, and the Railway Company receives only the ordinary railway fare.

It is clear that in this country of so-called equality, one thing that most strongly recommended the Pullman was the fact that it enabled the rich to create the clearest possible inequality in the conditions of even ordinary travel. The special luxury of the very rich is to have a special Pullman of their own, with sitting-rooms and bedrooms, rooms for servants, and, above all, suitable accommodation for your cook! This is the kind of thing that the Vanderbilts and Jay Goulds and Pullmans do in their own case.

I admit this is a long preamble to my visit to Pullman.

The second in command at the Pullman Company
(now a limited company) is Robert Caird, brother to
Mrs. Thomas Threlfall, to whom I had a letter of
introduction. Nothing could exceed his kindness.
He brought us down to Pullman, gave us lunch, took
us over the works, explained the history of the place,
and finally sent us on our journey to the northwest,
rejoicing, and furnished free with best Pullman tickets
as far as St. Paul and Minneapolis on the Mississippi River!

The history of Pullman City is indeed remarkable.
In 1880 there were not ten houses to be seen within
sight of what is now a town of about 3,000 inhabitants. The greater number of the inhabitants are
work people, at the manufactory of railway cars, of
which of all kinds (including the famous Pullman
sleeping-cars) a greater number is made than in any
works in the world—probably in any three or four
like works. The city is built, and I may add, gov-
erned upon the highest principle of parental government, a system of government not generally in favour. Here it is, and it ought to be in favour, for the
greatest regard has been had to the health, improvement, and amusements of the people. There is a
theatre, billiard-room, reading-, book-, lending library, savings bank, . . . put together. Excellent
and neat dwelling-houses at moderate rents for the

men furnished with all reasonable modern appliances
of comfort, and all of health.

It is, in truth, a model town. Wages all round
are high, and the lady who presides over the lend-
ing-library has a hundred dollars a month, equal to
about £200 a year of our money. A good many of
the men are Irish, but not the best paid, in other
words, not the doers of the best skilled work.

WEDNESDAY, AUGUST 29, 1883.

LEFT Chicago at 12.30 for St. Paul and Minneapolis and arrived at about 6 o'clock, A.M. The
journey was uneventful and nothing very startling,
till we crossed the Mississippi River. It is certainly
a grand volume of water, greater than anything we
can show, until our rivers gain breadth and dignity
from the sea; but still I was disappointed. I expected
something even greater and grander. No doubt,
when we recross it some 500 miles farther south, on
our way home, it will fully come up to my expecta-
tions. St. Paul and Minneapolis are both built on
the river, which is navigable for ships up to St. Paul.
The river is a great transport agency, not only for
river steamships and vessels, but also for the most
enormous lumber (that is, timber) rafts, which float
literally several thousand miles. Minneapolis is famous for its milling and its flour. The mills are
worked by the water-power of the Mississippi, which

is said for this purpose to be the finest in the world. The flour, too, is largely imported into England and Ireland, and its excellence is owing to the super-excellence of the wheat grown in and along the valley of this great river.

You see on all sides of you at the small railway depots great elevator grain stores, in which are loaded the grain bought from the farmers all round by the local agent of the big millers in the big towns.

Part of the district we traversed to-day had a perfectly English rural look at places—comfortabl(homesteads and well-tilled land. At other places the lands for miles are tenantless and left as the waters of the great flood left them. I could not help thinking that the crush and struggle for life in some small corners of the earth ought not to be as severe as they are, and that they would not be if only men knew better the uncrowded places ready to receive them, and ready to give up wholesome plenty at but small labour and entreaty.

Two things I have not yet seen, this side of the Atlantic: a really big tree and a mountain. Not that the country is not here and there fairly well wooded, but the timber is not of great growth; and not that the land is flat, for the places are after all few where you do not see from your carriage window undulations pleasant to the eye to dwell upon.

THURSDAY, AUGUST 30, 1883.

To-DAY for the first time we saw between Minne-apolis and St. Vincent a prairie stretching away in all directions, an unbroken, tenantless plain—perfectly level, on which (but for the tape-line of the railway) the hand of man had never laboured. It is certainly, if not a striking, a very suggestive sight.

At one or two places, say at Carlisle and at Rothesay, a very different sight was to be seen. Here the land had a well-cultivated appearance; in some fields the steam-reaper was at work; in others the men and women were building up the sheaves into stacks; in others the steam-plough was already at work, breaking up the land for the spring wheat, which is the best and fetches the highest prices. Here is a curious fact—curious at least to me. The wheat is sown in the end of August or beginning of September, and it has got a few inches above the ground when the hard weather sets in. In England this would generally be fatal; the frost nips the early vegetation. But in America the snow covers it up and shields it until the opening of spring, when the heat melts the protecting snow-cover and affords to the ground and the young vegetation the very moisture which they want.

We stayed at St. Paul only long enough to have a fair survey of the city, and then on again, and finally via St. Vincent, Emerson, and St. Boniface we reached Winnipeg at 6.30 A.M. (Friday). From Chicago to this place the distance is between 700 and 800 miles.

WINNIPEG, FRIDAY, AUGUST 31, 1883.

WINNIPEG is a town only about four years old and has now between 25,000 and 30,000 people in it! It has the marks of a new town in every way, just as the new American towns have. Fine wide streets, irregular houses, a fine brick building side by side with a wooden shanty, always dirty, muddy, unpaved streets, and a half-wild, half-tamed look about it! We are going to drive presently, and I must break off.

I have not altered my watch since I sailed from Liverpool—an age since! It will give Eily some idea of how far west we have got to say that while at Winnipeg the true sun-time is about 11.50 A.M., in London the true sun-time as by my watch is 5.40 P.M. You, Madam, and Clara, will be drinking your afternoon tea about the time that we are rising from a late breakfast.

WINNIPEG, SATURDAY, SEPT. 1, 1883.

WE spent the day very pleasantly. Mr. C. R. Brydges, the Land Commissioner of the Hudson Bay Company, at once called on us and arranged our day for us in a very agreeable way.

First, I went to his office and had a long and inter-

esting talk about the affairs of the Company. He
looks upon the shares as being intrinsically worth the
high prices (up to £39 and £40) paid last year for
them. He thinks that in ten or fifteen years the capital will be reduced by repayments from land sales to
a nominal amount, and that, too, without substan-
tially reducing the land-holding of the company. He
thinks the great "boom" of last year in land was very
injurious to Winnipeg, but that the town is sure from
its situation and the rich lands which surround it to
acquire a great position. In answer to my objection
that the Canadian Pacific with its twenty-five millions of acres and the North West Land Company,
with its five million acres (to say nothing of smaller
land companies and of the government land), would
be greatly in the way of the Hudson Company in their
sales, he said that was so, but that the Hudson
Company had an honourable tradition behind them;
that they sold on uniform, generally known terms;
that their title was clear; that they insisted on no conditions as to settlement or the breaking up of the
land—in fine, that the Hudson *did* sell, and *did* sell
almost preferentially to the other companies. He
complained that a good deal of the land round Winnipeg had got into the hands of speculators who were
holding for the rise, instead of putting it into market
or cultivating it.

As to the Canadian Pacific Railway Company, he
thinks it will have an important effect in opening up

Northwest Canada; but he seems by no means clear
that the line will pay its shareholders. He thinks
that after passing Brandon, the line by going farther
north than it does would have followed the fertile
land, whereas in its present direction westward it
crosses what he contends is the American desert,
which he says is to be found continued in Texas,
Arizona, etc.

We saw a good deal of the town, which is very interesting. Here you may see the town growing under your eyes—the very prairie being trodden down
into the semblance of a new street, while a hundred
yards farther stands a building of a most imposing
kind, such as would not disgrace Manchester or
Liverpool. In the unoccupied places wooden shanties
are erected by temporary dwellers—tradesmen who
are for the time working in the town; farmers or intending farmers who have not yet settled their loca-
tion west or northwest. Good masons are getting
about $3 a day—equal to about 12s. 6d. English
money. Carpenters are getting about the same. The
price of a shave is from 15 to 25 cents, i.e., from 8d.
to 1s. However, it is to be added that these high
prices do not hold all the year round.

We visited Portage la Prairie, which is about 50
miles from Winnipeg and on the Canadian Pacific
Railway.

It is greatly inferior to Winnipeg in size and in
every other respect. It, too, has recently sprung up.

We got a carriage here and drove miles out of the town to see the recent settlements on the prairie, and this was a sight of the very greatest interest to me.

As a matter of picturesqueness I am disappointed in the prairie. There is a certain attractiveness in the flat uniform richness of the landscape covered with a golden wheat harvest—and a pleasant suggestiveness of rude comfort and plenty; but it is dull, very dull. Not a mountain, nor even a hill to be seen— as smooth as the calm sea and as flat. Except in the neighbourhood of the rivers, there are no trees to be seen, and even these do not appear to acquire any great height. The absence of the trees is a curable matter, and already one sees signs of planting in and about the houses which promise speedily to add some diversity to the landscape as well as afford to the homesteads valuable protection against the fierce winter winds, which at times sweep across the plains with a fury almost resistless.

The houses are all of wood, and none of them large. The majority of the settlers here are Scotch, and, while the land seems fairly well tilled, there is not much attempt at neatness in their gardens, offices, yards, or houses. But *all* whom we have yet seen in Canada seem well fed and well clad. Except amongst some wretched Indians there is not the slightest appearance of want. As Martin remarked yesterday while watching the children file out of the school, "Not a darned stocking on one of them!"

About five miles from Portage we went into the house of one Woods. His father bought some years ago 160 acres of land partly in cultivation, paying $3½ an acre, equal to $560, or in English money to £112. In the kitchen the dinner was on the table. A great appetising dish of ham and eggs flanked by beer-jugs and vegetable marrows, cabbage and potatoes. In the yard was a lot of poultry—geese, turkeys, ordinary fowls, also pigs and a dozen milch cows. His family consisted of two brothers and two sisters and a couple of servants, and when asked what he did with his fowls, eggs, pigs, butter, milk, etc., his invariable answer, given with a satisfied chuckle, was "Eat 'em."

Now this was a case in which the land had been bought, but the Dominion Government gives 160 acres for $10, if within a fixed number of years the farmer settling breaks up a certain number of acres for arable purposes! Just think of this, and then of the miserable patches of wretched land on which the Irish peasant so often tries to make out a living! The two difficulties are fuel and the winters. The former difficulty will, it is believed, speedily disappear, as coal or a superior lignite is supposed to be plentiful in Canada; and this will of course go greatly to mitigate the winter's severity. The winters, although severe, tested by temperature (frequently 30° below zero),

are very dry and bracing, and several people tell me
are not to be compared in discomfort to a severe
muggy winter in England.

In our drive we visited two encampments of Indians with their tepees or tents in the open plain.
They were of two tribes—the Objibaways and the
Sues (I am not sure of my orthography). The former are said to be a harmless race and to be native in
the country. The Sues came to Canada across the
American frontier, after having (it is said) perpe-
trated a series of atrocities in Minnesota. This about
a dozen years since. The native Indians are treated
very kindly by the Government. They are falling
away (but not very rapidly) before the advance of
what the Whites call civilisation; and the Government reserves certain districts for them and also supplies them with a certain amount of food. They are
generally well spoken of, and one of the oldest of the
Hudson Bay Agents told me that, so long as faith
was kept with them, they kept faith. Their tents are
wretched in the extreme. Blankets to lie upon and
some wood to cook their food, but no sign of stores
of food or drink or clothes. To a slight extent they
are absorbed by the white population; and, as half-
breeds, some of them rise to power and distinction.
Indeed the present Prime Minister of the Province of
Manitoba—Mr. Knockway—is a half-breed. The
Sues are physically not inferior to Whites as to size,
muscularity, etc., the others decidedly inferior.

On Saturday evening we dined at the Manitoba Club as guests at a dinner given to Mr. Archibold (a cousin of the late Mr. Justice Archibold), who was on a visit here, but who was the first Lieutenant-Governor of Manitoba. The speeches were to me most interesting. The ex-Governor gave an account of his first entry into Winnipeg in 1870 (exactly thirteen years ago), when his journey from Montreal occupied twenty-six days and when the census of Winnipeg then taken showed seventy houses and a population of about 350! Now the population is between 25,-000 and 30,000, and you can get from Montreal in about 48 hours!

SUNDAY, SEPT. 2, 1883.

AT THE Saturday's dinner we made the acquaintance of the Catholic Archbishop Tache—a Frenchman —who was one of the most honoured guests at the banquet. There was also the Protestant Bishop—a Doctor Macrae. They seem to get on remarkably well; there is no religious bickering, and even on the vexed question of education they pull together. There is a University of Manitoba which is merely an examining and degree-granting body (as distinguished from a teaching body), upon the Board of Directors of which each religious body has fair representation. The Archbishop is a remarkable man. He has made many missions amongst the Indians and has effected large conversions amongst them. He, too, speaks

well of them, and says they are difficult to deal with
only when they get contaminated by admixture with
the Whites! To-day we went to High Mass at his
church, St. Boniface—the name of the place and of
the church—and heard a French sermon. St. Boniface is across the Red River over against Winnipeg.
It is a French Settlement, and to this day the school
lessons are taught alternately in French and in English! It was quite curious to notice in the village the
French surnames as well as the French names descriptive of the particular business carried on: "Epicier,"
"charcutier," etc. I see I have not mentioned one
main peculiarity of the prairie land, which renders it
so easy of cultivation. Stones are almost unknown in
it! Fancy this in view of the braes of Killowen! The
plough runs without let or hindrance through a black
mould varying in thickness from two to eight feet.
So rich is the land that so far manure is unnecessary,
though it must in time be used, and in some places the
same crop has year after year without rest or inter-
ruption been taken out of the land. This, however,
is considered a too exhaustive and an unwise system
to pursue.

MONDAY, SEPT. 3, 1883.

THIS evening we start for Glyndon right south (retracing our steps) and then go on to Fargo on
the Northern Pacific line, where we hope to join the
great Villard Excursion Party on their way to the
Pacific Ocean at Portland.

WILLIAM M. EVARTS

TUESDAY, SEPT. 4, 1883.

L AST night we left Winnipeg by the evening train, and travelling via Emerson, St. Vincent, and Glyndon, arrived at Fargo, a station on the Northern Pacific Line. At Emerson we were joined by the Hon. Broderick, M.P. for a division of Surrey (son of Lord Middleton).

We reached Fargo at 8 o'clock and found the place *en fête* in expectation of the arrival of the excursion trains carrying the Villard party.

The only thing noticeable about the decorations was that they were formed from the products of the district, wheat, oats, Indian corn, and so forth. There were in all four trains, on the first of which were our host Villard, President of the Northern Pacific Railway, Sir James Hannen and Lord Justice Bowen. No. 1 train was bang full, and our directions were to get into the first train in which there was room; but it was found there would not be room until No. 4 arrived.

However, No. 2 duly arrived and we were promptly admitted and found ourselves amongst friends, viz.—Grey, M.P. (not Gray), Henry Edwards, M.P., Horace Davey, M.P., Q.C., W. M. Evarts (the Leader of the U. S. Bar), Rev. Stemthall (Manchester), Bruce (Engineer, London), Samuelson, Jr., M.P., Buxton, M.P., Bryce, M.P. The swell of our party is Grant (General Ulysses), who was, as you know, twice President of the U. S. At every station he is the centre of attraction. Occasionally he gives them a word or two—no more—but generally the proceedings begin and end with hand-shaking—the little ones being lifted up to touch the hand of their great General. There is some genuine interest about Grant, but no enthusiasm such as we understand it; but Americans tell me it is a weakness they do not indulge in. Every place we come to is gay with flags, triumphal arches, sentences of welcome in mammoth letters, made of flowers, sheaves of grain, etc. "Welcome Villard," "The capital city (of the particular State) welcomes President Villard's guests," and so on.

At most of the towns, big and little, a troupe of well-dressed little girls rush into the carriages with bouquets of flowers for each traveller.

What greatly impresses me is the harmonious way in which *all* seem to join in making the whole affair "run," as they call it. I have not noticed a policeman taking any part whatever in the order of proceedings; and, looking at the crowd, it is impossible to do as you can in England so easily—distinguish classes. They are all one class and even in the style and manner of dress—except when in actual working clothes —there is but little difference.

I ought earlier to have mentioned in reference to General Grant that, noticing his apparent popularity I asked whether he was a likely candidate for the next Presidency. The answer (and that by a friend of his) was, "No, he was suspected of corruption when in office, and is not trusted." It is *very* curious to note that no public man is free from this imputation of corruption in popular opinion—whether he be a political person or merely president of a railroad or of any other public company. Even judges and juries are accused of corruption, and certainly at times justly accused. It is the worst trait I notice in the national character that these things are mentioned with a shrug and a grin—as if they must be, and the men engaged in them are not, when detected, overwhelmed with contempt and disgrace as they commonly would be with us. It is common, too, to hear speech of the bribery of the members of the local Legislatures and governing bodies and even of the United States legislative body. Since the days of Walpole this has been unknown (at least in the grosser mode) in England —except in a few notable instances.

BISMARCK, WEDNESDAY, SEPT. 5, 1883.

OUR yesterday's journey extended from Fargo to the town (Bismarck), which is the capital of the corn-growing State of Dakota. The considerable places we passed were Tower City, Valley City, Jamestown, Cleveland, Crystal Springs, Sterling, and Clarke.

Near Tower City we had what might, with less

care than they exercise here, have been a serious acci-
dent. We have two engines to our train (No. 2) and
the axle-tree of the tender of the second of the engines
broke right in two from some flaw in the iron. This
was discovered in time to prevent the chance of the
engines leaving the line—indeed the passengers in the
train did not know that anything untoward had happened until the train stopped.

The delay of a couple of hours was a great delight
to many. It would have been to you, Madam, if you
had been here, and to you, Rosa, especially, and above
all to you, May. We were in the middle of the unbroken prairie—several miles from the nearest town
or indeed dwelling-place: the weather was delicious,
the air crisp and delightfully bracing—the sun shining brightly and the great world of prairie flowers
(and botanists say it *is* a great world) giving forth
for the occasion all their beauty and all their fra-
grance.

There are some three or four ladies of the party,
and these and several of the gentlemen set themselves
in a determined way to make a specimen-collection. I
am not as you know, Madam, learned in such matters,
but I will venture to beg your gracious acceptance of
the enclosed sample of the wild rose of the American
prairie.

It was very amusing to note that, although the
scene of our disaster was remote from the busy haunts
of men and women, yet very soon after it happened

vehicles were to be seen converging to us from all directions across the prairie. Their occupants, ladies and gentlemen, would not disgrace Regent Street in the season. But I think this full-dress appearance was to be accounted for by the fact that the settlers were on their way to greet us in the nearest town. We reached Bismarck about 2 this morning—sleeping in the cars. Under the circumstances the night was as pleasant as could be expected, but certainly not so pleasant as the day. The members of the party move freely from carriage to carriage along the whole length of the train, chatting pleasantly. Then some write, some read, some play whist (very bad whist) and so the day passes quickly along. To-day there was some serious work to do in Bismarck. Mrs. Villard was to lay the foundation-stone of the capitol here in the capital city of the State, and accordingly we were ordered to be in line by six o'clock. A great procession formed and proceeded in great state and with every variety of equipage to the *locus in quo*. (Frank will, if needful, translate.)

I did not go: the proceedings are now going on as I write. What is *now?* Well, I will tell you. I have not altered my watch since I sailed from Liverpool, and I am pretty well able to tell at any given moment what you are all about—whether getting up or going to bed, sitting down to breakfast or rising from the dinner-table. As I write, it is with you about 4.30 P.M., and Clara is beginning to think it is time Gass

brought her afternoon tea. Here, by the sun's true
time, it is not quite 10 A.M.! I am of course getting
farther behind you as I get more and more westward.
What the difference will be when I get to Portland
and San Francisco I don't know; but I will note and
tell you.

(Frank! Be good enough to explain for the benefit
of your younger brother and of your younger sisters
the principle on which time is reckoned with reference
to the sun, and further explain how starting from
Rostrevor as a fixed point you get before that time if
you go east, and fall behind it as you go west. Do this
in a few lucid sentences, intelligible to the meanest
comprehension.)

The sight (or the sights) of this morning was the
famous Sitting Bull, the Chief of the Sioux Indians.
(By the way, I have previously spelt this by sound
and incorrectly.) I shook hands (as part of the pro-
gramme) with the old ruffian. It was he who in Minnesota and Dakota cut to pieces a number of American soldiers a few years ago under command of a
dashing cavalry officer called Colonel-General Custer.
After this business a number of the Sioux crossed the
border (as I think I have already mentioned) into
Canada. He is a remarkable looking man. He is
medium height and broad-shouldered. His face is
certainly fine, and his eyes large, dark-coloured, and
thoughtful. His forehead is broad and low—certainly a clever head and take him altogether I should

SITTING BULL

certainly not set him down as a cruel or cold-blooded man. He wore a crucifix round his neck; but the superintendent who acted as translator did not seem to think that there was much real significance in this Christian and Catholic emblem. By a curious custom amongst the Sioux the men anoint their hair and plait it while the women allow it to hang dishevelled on their shoulders.

I must here note, while it is in my mind, a remarkable characteristic of all the towns and cities *however new* on this great continent (I include Canada). It is this: They have amongst them (even when their streets are not properly made and when they are deficient in many of the commonest conveniences in old places) all the very latest inventions. Thus in every business place of any pretensions, in most professional men's houses, and in many private houses there is electric light. One lady at Winnipeg informed me she always ordered from her butcher and other tradespeople by telephone. Do not tell this to Mrs. Fryer (who is, I hope, very well) or she will be wanting it in Harley Street! Again, the electric light is not uncommonly to be found in towns of a population of 2,000 or 3,000. At Fargo they had an electric light fixed about sixty feet high, which is visible forty miles off and by which (they say) you can read a quarter of a mile off. At Bismarck there was a strong illustration of this early goaheadness. Fire is a great enemy whom they dread, looking to the easily ignitible character of their buildings and in some places their scant supply of water. You find, therefore, their Fire Salvage Department well organised in every town; but in Bismarck they have got what I suppose is hardly or but little known in England, namely, a chemical fire engine directed to the extinguishment of fire by means which its name indicates.

THURSDAY, SEPT. 6, 1883.
(*En route*)

I WISH to begin to-day's note by a word of apology to Sitting Bull. I am told by well-informed Americans that S. B. is *not* the ruffian I have called him, and that the better opinion now is that he was not guilty of any unwarlike or treacherous conduct in relation to the defeat of General Custer's force, which was fairly met by S. B. in the open, but met by a vastly superior force to that of the American General.

There is little to say descriptive of Bismarck. Describe one of the new cities of the States, and you have described all.

The presence of the Celtic-Irish element speedily showed itself in one who boldly announced himself as a vendor of "Krubeens." I should not be surprised, Madam, if (notwithstanding your well-known national feeling) it were necessary to explain that this means "pig's feet." One other Irish item. A grand printed notice, obviously official, announced that all who helped the great show deserved to be encouraged, *but* all who did not were to be "boycotted"! There is obviously no Coercion Act in force here.

A little out of order I want to record the first place in which I saw a hill, or, as they call them, "Bluff." As we approached Valley City, a low range of hills appeared and were as grateful to my eye, tired of the monotonous prairie, as water to the thirsty palate. But these hills have a special importance in the conformation of the country. They are, in fact, the dividing line of two great water sheds. It is startling, but it is true, that the waters falling to the east of them find their way after thousands of miles to Hudson Bay and the Gulf of Saint Lawrence and those falling to the west to the great rivers of the south and the Gulf of Mexico.

Outside Bismarck and within half a mile of the town we cross the mighty Missouri. You recollect Henry Russell's song; I've not heard it since I was a boy:

"To the West, to the West, to the Land of the Free,
Where mighty Missouri rolls down to the sea,
Where a man is a man if he's willing to toil
And the humblest may gather the fruits of the soil."

Well, Missouri *is* a mighty but it is also a muddy river. The water is now low, but the brown devastating mark of the winter's flood is to be seen high and far up on the banks, forcibly suggesting what it may be at its best or worst.

From this the country is to the eye, and in fact, less rich in pasture and less cultivated, and bluffs are to be found in all directions rising suddenly, apparently, from the plain graced now and then, but sparsely, with trees.

At little Missouri we came upon scenery really grand. I am poor at description. Imagine an amphitheatre of mountains rising precipitously from the level of the railway track which winds around their base for more than the semicircle. Imagine a flat plain inside the circle—flat and monotonous with one great exception. Right in the centre of the circle rises a bluff higher than the rest, standing alone—its summit a great plateau and its base washed by the little Missouri. I was startled when asked to ride up and down this great stone castle, but like several others I got on a wiry mustang pony and very soon found myself climbing something very like a wall. Coming down was even worse, and I should not be at all inclined to repeat the ride. But I must say the view from the plateau was very fine and was a specimen of scenery new to me. The sides of the hills were completely denuded of all clay by the fierce rains of the winter and spring and yet vegetation of varied tints clung to their sides, and, bathed in the rich glow of the approaching sunset, presented a marvellous bit of glorious colouring. At our feet the little Missouri lay, and but for the presence in one spot of our train —itself a summary of the material civilisation of nineteen centuries—we could truly say we looked upon the scene exactly as it appeared to the Crowfeet Indians or other aboriginal inhabitants before the aggressive foot of the white man was ever planted upon it.

Close by, a *certain* Marquis—son of the Duke of Vallombrosa (it is said)—has established a great cattle ranch. A month ago an attack was made upon him by the cowboys or cattle herds whose interests he was supposed to be affecting. He shot one mortally and maimed two others: since which his days have been peace. He is a finer looking man and bigger than Parnell, but reminded me and others of the latter. At 6 o'clock this morning (I was up at 5.30) we reached the Yellowstone River and for miles our track ran so close to its banks that I could almost dip a long stick into the bright clear water—for the water was bright and clear. Indeed it is the first river which was not muddy and which can boast a pebbly bank. Some of these reaches in the early morning sunlight looked perfectly lovely. On one side of the train the bluffs lifted their heads; on the other ran the river. The flat spaces at the base of the bluffs and sometimes lying between them are, it appears, by some geologists accounted for thus: They allege that the intervening spaces were originally deposits of coal or of lignite, and that in some great incendiary act of Nature they were destroyed.

At 10.30 A.M. to-day (Thursday) we reached

Billings, where I now write. Billings is another mushroom city in the United States of which geographers knew nothing until, I believe, about two years ago! It is already one of the principal towns of the State of Montana (the capital town is Helena), which State is reputed of enormous natural resources. Again and again the thought is thrust upon me, in view of all the wide unoccupied expanse of rich land, *why* there should be such a crush and struggle for a corner in a squalid town or on a bleak sterile hillside? I do not shut my eyes to the fact that love of place of birth is an important factor, but it may have, after all, an exaggerated importance given to it.

FRIDAY, SEPT. 7, 1883.

(Fifth Despatch. *En route* Livingstone to Helena)

THE charm and interest of our excursion seem to vary and intensify from day to day.

Yesterday the leading incident in our proceedings was perfectly unique. Never again probably will such a sight be seen as we saw yesterday at Graycliff.

Graycliff is on the borders of the Crow Indians' reservation, which comprises the enormous space of 200 square miles. It had been arranged with their chiefs, who are, and have now for years been friendly with the Whites, that a great assembly of their tribes should take place in celebration of the opening of this great trans-continental line. Such an assembly has not been seen since in their war paint they some years back made their last stand for the land from which the murderous and civilising White sought to expel them. Their efforts were fruitless, and they fell back before a civilisation which came to them heralded by bloodshed and rapine. It is perhaps hardly to be wondered at that under such circumstances they did not feel attracted to the manners and customs of their conquerors.

Since then they have been practically pensioners of the United States Government which grants them this large reserve and besides supplies them with food. They do no regular work. The reserve is little better than a poor-house from which they will assuredly be expelled as soon as the necessity if not the convenience of the all-grasping white man requires it.

Fenimore Cooper has invested the American Indians with Spartan qualities and virtues and with a simple dignity and grace peculiarly attractive. If his descriptions were true and did not originate in his own poetic mind, the Indians of to-day are greatly degenerate. On the whole, it is conceded that in this, as in every conflict between the interests of the aborigines and the invading Whites, the former have been unjustly treated and have cruelly suffered, and it may well be that contact and conflict with the subduing Whites have lost them their best characteristics and that they have acquired in exchange the worst qualities of their conquerors. Certainly to-day reliable opinion does not strongly pronounce for them.   Parents love their children, but children do not equally love their parents, and a son is not supposed to be undutiful if he leaves his aged mother to die in the shelter of a tree, and modestly supplied with water and the sweet root of the camus.   They degrade their womenkind, whom they treat as fit only to be hewers of wood and drawers of water.   It used to be said that the Indian children suffered pain and showed it not.   Well, I can vouch for the fact that, when yesterday at Graycliff a chubby Indian boy of about six years trod on the prickly cactus, he bellowed with a vigour which—well, any little boy of my acquaintance could not surpass.

I find I have been moralising lengthily and prosily.

The tribes inhabiting the Crow reservation were to exhibit to their quondam enemies the war dances with which they had been wont to excite their warriors before battle against their spectators of to-day. There was something to me peculiarly melancholy and saddening in the exhibition—these men degrading their rites and humbling their mighty chiefs (some of them with the mark of the white man on his forehead) to make an American holiday.   But here—I am moralising again.

I wish some one with an eye to colours and detail and withal some power of description had yesterday been in my place.   You, Madam, or you, Rosa, or you, Clara, or you, Eily.

GATHERING OF CROW INDIANS

As we approached Graycliff, we were struck by the array of horses grazing on the plain, numbering several thousand and certainly exceeding the number of the tribe, which was computed at 2,500. Nearer still to the town appeared many hundred tepee tents presenting in shelter of the bluffs, which formed a harmonious background for them, a striking and peculiar picture. Close by, many of the old, very old squaws, sat on their hunkers—weird, wrinkled, impassive, and, it may be added, filthy. Here and there the little ones appeared, some of them really handsome, with faces as impassive almost as those of the old crones.

Close by the town, but on the unbroken prairie, was the focus point of attraction. The people of the district for miles round had gathered in, dressed in their best and showing off in their best teams. The Indians had already formed themselves in a semicircle, some standing, some sitting, some lying lazily and dreamily on the ground, some on horseback, and all dressed in their most fantastic dresses and painted in their most fantastic colours. But this applies only to the men of the tribe; the squaws, huddled together, looked moodily on. The resources of the tribe in the matter of adornment were exhausted on the chiefs, for the women were dirty, squalid, and showed no sign of even passing comeliness except in the case of two or three of the very young girls amongst them.

But what is this horrible row? It is the full choral

strength of the Crow-foots in the air. The band sat
in a semicircle apart, beating drums, its members apparently vieing with one another in the production of
the most discordant conglomeration of sounds I ever
listened to. It seemed to rouse the performers to activity. The master of ceremonies—whose face was
cross-barred in yellow and black with a fantastic
headdress and a gorgeous tail made up principally of
peacocks' feathers and the management of which required a good deal of care—now stirred about
amongst the chiefs and selected the performers for
the opening dance. It requires a person with some
imagination like you, Rosa, to give a graceful description of what to my prosaic eye seemed ungraceful in
the extreme—striking, fantastic, unique but still ungraceful.

A hideous dish of cooked dog's meat was placed in
the centre and round it the chiefs performed what
was described as a religious rite with excited gesticu-
lation and most uncouth utterance. Presently the
music became more discordant than ever, and now the
dancers gathered more energy of voice and limb, and
are supposed to be shadowing forth and inspiriting to
deeds of danger. This was the war dance. Later
there came love dances (still confined to men) whose
meaning one could not, without help, guess. I removed to a distance on a slope, and shutting one's
ears to sound and sufficiently far off not to observe
the disagreeableness of the Indians, the scene was as-

suredly of a striking kind—the beauty of the place, the glory of the setting sun, the bright colouring, the fantastic movements and the commanding figures of the Indians side by side with the men of the White race—all combined to form a picture such as will probably never again be seen. Here were the representatives of an old dynasty which was almost dead, and, close by, in the luxurious steam equipage (a compendium of the material civilisation of nineteen centuries) the successful invader, the ruthless, aggressive, all-conquering white man.

These were some of the notions which crowded in upon me while we rolled away from Graycliff, as the sun went down.

Between Graycliff and Livingstone in the night we lost some fine scenery. Dimly in the night I saw the outline of the Crazy Range with its leading mountain, called "Old Baldy."

LIVINGSTONE, FRIDAY, SEPT. 7, 1883.

WHEN I looked out of my berth at 5 o'clock A.M. this morning, close upon us was a noble range of hills which reminded me forcibly of the Mourne Mountains—the chief amongst these being Sugar-loaf, shaped like Slieve Donard. It is this which is called "Old Baldy." We are here at the gate of the wonderful Yellowstone country in which the American people are reserving as a national playground a

space some 3,000 miles square at an altitude of some
7,000 or 8,000 feet above sea level, and filled with
wondrous natural points of interest.   It is intended on
the return journey to spend two or three days specially
at this point; but as I go to San Francisco and home
by a line farther south this pleasure will not be open
to me.

In December, 1882, there were not fifty people in
Livingstone.   To-day the population is 2,500 and
there are baths, banks, concert halls, and a skating
rink!   The electric light and the telephone are, of
course, here.

Before the morning dew had been dried up, we
started to make the ascent of the great spur which
prepares us for the still greater rise, a little further
on, of the great Rockies themselves.

So gradual has been our ascent that it is startling to
be reminded that at Livingstone we are 4,500 feet
above sea level.

This eccentric line represents very closely the *pro-
file* of the line of ascent we have to make.   I need not
say that the principle of the inclined plane (explain,
Cyril, for May's benefit) is largely brought into
requisition; but that makes our progress all the more
interesting, for we wind round and round the mountains and looking up their sides we see the made road-
way we have to traverse terraced high above our
heads.

As we go up a steep incline (about 1 in 30), our

train parts in two; but the automatic brake instantly stops the downward descent of the part left behind, and the engine quietly and safely backs to recouple it.

Should a breakdown of a serious kind occur, they have the instant means of communicating with any part of the world for help. How? You may well ask, for we are often miles away from human dwelling-places, and the only thing which seems to hold us to the world of men is the single wire of the telegraph which accompanies us even in our greatest solitude. But of what avail is the telegraph, for it is miles before we can reach a telegraph station? Ingenuity, however, has even overcome that difficulty. With each train is an electric battery, and with each battery a clerk able to operate, who by simply hooking on to the single wire is literally in communication with all the world.

At last we reach the city of Bozeman—verily a city —5,714 ft. above the level of the sea, and an old city, too, as things go here, for it is upwards of ten years old. Between this spur which we have surmounted and the Rockies lies the valley of the Upper Missouri, fertile in a high degree and singularly beautiful in places. The Missouri, which you will recollect, we met before more than once, is here nearer its source—indeed it is the junction of the rivers Gallatin, Madison and Jefferson which here first take that name—and it is as yet uncontaminated by contact with the populous haunts of men. On either side of it the mountains rise, well clad even to their very tops, often sheer up from the plain, whose richness of soil contrasts strongly with the sterile, rockbound character of the hills.

It is notable that in the upper part of this valley, between five and six thousand feet above the sea, the crops are remarkable for their abundance and yield. I had here (at Bozeman) a few words with Pat Brady, who works on the N. P. R. Company. He is from County Armagh (my own county[1]) and has been in the United States ten years. He was well fed and clad and content. He enquired with interest about Ireland; but when I asked him whether he would like to go back, he answered with a grin that he would not mind, but he would require to be furnished with a return ticket to the United States before leaving them.

Our journey for the rest of the day was for the greater part along the Missouri, and finally the four sections or divisions of which the Excursion Party is made halted at a place called Butler, a little way up the great and final ascent of the Rockies.

This halt was a pleasant incident. It afforded friends separated in the actual journey the pleasant opportunity of intercourse.

[1]Ballybot is on the Armagh side of Newry

SATURDAY, SEPT. 8, 1883.

AT 5.30 we left Butler for the final ascent. The morning is lovely. Everything looking its best— though indeed my American friends say spring is *the* time to realise the full beauty of this region. The scenery was what I understand by "Alpine" in its character and the air sharp, cold, clear, and bracing —had a peculiarly exhilarating effect.

In advance, often miles off, we could see the trestle bridges over which we had to cross. Several of these are above 60 feet high: they are all made of wood: none of them are built on piles let into the ground; and at a distance they present a very fragile, spidery (is this adjective allowable?) appearance. Mr. Bruce, C.E., and General Hutchinson, however, said they were really very strong and showed very skilful work. Up, up we go, slowly but surely, the very engine seeming by its heavy pulsations to express its sense of the difficulty before us. Some of us notice a well-defined track which we cross and recross and never get far away from at this particular place. What is it, think you? Originally an Indian trail, it was used for years and years by the agents of the Hudson Bay Company, and formed part of a road some 600 miles long or so from Port Benton on the Missouri in the east to Walla-Walla (now a station on the Northern Pacific Railway) in the west. What a history is involved in the sight of these two roadways side by side—so different in character, but whose identity of track and direction evidenced the wise observation of our forefathers in times so much less advanced in science than these.

About two miles short of the summit several of us elected to walk on in advance of the first section of our train and we were well repaid. Walking the open trestle bridges was not pleasant, though not at all dangerous, so long as you keep a cool head; but the sense of active motion, the fresh glow it brought, the delightful view all round, and the anticipation that in a few minutes we should have reached "tip-top" and, turning our back on the east, be looking for the first time down on the Pacific slopes—all combined to give us a keen sense of enjoyment.

Up we go, winding in and out of the mountains; make a final bend; know we are then 5,813 feet above ocean level and that the vast extent of land that opens before us in valley and hill, in river and in forest, leads us to the great Pacific! Here is the dividing line in the watershed between east and west—which determines what water shall lose itself in the immensity of the Atlantic and what in the Pacific Seas. Still, I may as well incidentally mention we are still about a thousand miles from the most westerly point of our journey, although we are about 1,200 miles west of Lake Superior! Just recall, Frank, the distance from Kinsale Head to the Giant's Causeway,

and it will perhaps help you to realise what these distances mean!

We reached the summit about 8.30 A.M., and at
11.15 we struck the river known as Clark's Fork, an
important tributary of the Columbia River, which,
however, only assumes its great proportions and importance after it leaves the Lake Pend d'Oreille.
(See your maps; I will try and send one.) Clark deserves more than a passing word: it is after him that
the river is named. He and a man named Lewis at
the instance and expense of the United States Government of the day, from May, 1804 to September, 1806 were engaged in exploring the approach
from the east to the Pacific by a northern route
which this very day reached its completion! Their
story is full of interest, peril, and adventure.

After passing Garrison City, which is named after
President Villard's father-in-law, we reach the spot
(named at least for the day, "Spike Point") at which
the final spike is to be driven and the trains pass to
and fro for the first time on an unbroken continuous
line of railway communication from Lake Superior
in the east to Portland in the west. This point is
1,198 miles from Lake Superior and 847 from Puget
Sound. A large building had been erected for the
speakers and the more distinguished guests; and
round it, on the untilled ground, which has never yet
yielded to human labour, there were gathered together a motley but most interesting assemblage.

For miles round the settlers, farmers, traders, Indians, Governor, and other local authorities had come to assist at the completion of a great work which brought their country for the first time within civilised limits. All manner of equipage had been brought into requisition from the buggy and team which would not have disgraced Central Park, to the homely farming wagon filled with the settler's family group. There were inequalities of style, dress, and equipage amongst them, but there was no underfed or badly-clad man or woman to be seen in all the thousands. The order preserved was really remarkable—no crushing, hustling, or unseemly noises. Each one seemed to think that in some sort it concerned him that the proceedings should be seemly and in order.

I will not stop to describe the actual work of completion. In almost shorter time than I take to write it, a certain number of lengths of sleepers and rails were laid and spiked until the final spike alone remained to be driven. This done by President Villard, to whose energy and ability so much of the final success is by all attributed—guns were fired and huzzas sent up to celebrate the consummation. During all the preliminary proceedings I was most interested in Madam Villard (to whom I was to-day presented by my friend Dr. Borchardt of Manchester). She is the daughter of Mr. Garrison, who fought and suffered years back for the cause of the Negro. She is about forty years of age, pleasant of face, and neat

THE CELEBRATION AT SPIKE POINT

and graceful of figure. She is chatty and wholly un-affected. To-day when she was not engaged in inter-esting her guests her face wore an anxious expression, and I am sure that no one was more relieved than she when the complete success of the proceedings was fully assured.

But I have to do also with the speakers. There were famous men to speak, and I was anxious to have the benefit of a rare opportunity of listening to some American orators whose reputations stand very high.

President Villard read a very excellent speech, sound in sense and good in tone and taste, the effect of which would have been greatly increased could it have been spoken and not merely read. Then fol-lowed the man whom all the other American speak-ers concurred in calling (and they ought to know) the "great orator" of the day—I mean my friend, as I am glad to be able to call him, W. M. Evarts, Bar-rister. I made his acquaintance in London, now a good many years since, through the introduction of my distinguished and learned friend, Mr. J. P. Ben-jamin. Mr. Evarts is certainly a remarkable man. He is above sixty years of age, but his manner is vi-vacious and his tongue as ready as it was twenty years since—so say his friends and admirers. His head and face are striking and present a highly intellectual type of what we are in the habit of calling the Yankee. His effort was clearly to be the effort of the day. To him was assigned the part of historian and apologist of the Northern Pacific Line, and this was hardly a subject best fitted to illustrate his undoubtedly great powers of speech. But more. These are days in which you speak not so much to the audience facing you, as to that greater audience—if one may so call them—who are addressed through their morning paper. It was (as Mr. Evarts told me) a regrettable necessity that his speech was in print before he left New York, for otherwise it could not appear (as it did) *in extenso* the morning after its delivery in some 500 newspapers throughout the land. This circumstance certainly detracted from its effect. The effort to remember what had been written, and the frequent reference to the printed proof took away from the powerful oration that character of spontaneity which is one of the greatest charms of human utterance. Towards the end there were one or two passages of great dignity and power which suggested, if they did not quite realize, the grounds on which Mr. Evart's great reputation is based. His friends said it was not one of his happiest efforts, and they added that at this period of his history he is at his best when he is called upon for an impromptu speech and upon an occasion when he can give the reins to a pleasant wit and a caustic tongue. As a companion, I know no more agreeable man. Kindly, humorous, cheerful, and full of anecdote, personal and historical, spiced occasionally with just enough sarcasm to sharpen the palate—I know no one with whom I would rather travel on a long railway journey in an interesting country.

To him succeeded Mr. Teller, Secretary of the Interior under President Arthur. His effort was not a success. Good, earnest man, I doubt not, but he has studied in a school of oratory which savours more of the religious conventicle than of the legislative forum.

To him succeeded Mr. Billings, whose speech was · on the whole the greatest success of the day. Mr. Billings was formerly a lawyer practising in San Francisco. He afterwards took to commerce and was formerly President of the Northern Pacific Railway Company. His figure and face do not readily lend themselves to oratory; but, when he is fairly under way, you cease to criticise or to notice personal appearance. His language is forcible and copious, his manner impressive, and although one would be inclined to say there was exaggeration in his style, his earnestness impressed his auditors, and they were indeed fairly aroused, and for the first time in the proceedings, to enthusiasm.

To him succeeded Sir James Hannen as the first of the speakers representing the guests. He spoke for the English guests. Sir James Hannen is not an orator according to American ideas of oratory. There are no sonorous, high-swelling sentences, no studied risings or fallings of the voice, but there is exceedingly good taste, an appropriateness of language and a dignity of manner which together produce a most favourable and agreeable impression. It is, I think, to the credit of the good taste of our American friends that many of them considered Sir James Hannen's the best speech of the day.

Herr Gneist and Dr. Hoffman from Germany followed—the former a distinguished member of the German Parliament, and the latter a celebrated professor of chemistry. There was nothing to note in the speech of either—save that Dr. Hoffman in very bad taste indulged in sneers at the supposed miracles of the early and middle ages and said that this was the true age of miracles according to and not against the order of nature—such miracles, in fine, as the completion of the Great Northern Pacific Railway.

Then followed speeches from the Governors of the several States and Territories through which the line of railway runs. At this stage I began to tire of American oratory at best. We had in these speeches some of the worst characteristics, and none of the best, of American oratory. They were turgid, extravagant in language and sometimes in gesture, and seemed principally directed to claiming for their respective States the right to the title of Garden of Eden. One of them, however, reached the climax— the man from Washington Territory—when he told us that all the trees there were 250 feet high and at least five feet in circumference, and that his territory was the real centre of the United States.

At last a tiresome but very interesting day is

ended; and, as we walk back to our cars some way
from our focus point, there are returning, on this side
of Clark's Fork and on that, the happy settlers,
peaceably but merrily, and rejoicing that they have
assisted at a great national work—important to the
Nation, but specially important to them who for seed-
time and for harvest-time, for themselves and for
their children, have cast their lot in the Far West.

SUNDAY, SEPT. 9, 1883.

AFTER the successful ceremonial of yesterday we
continued our way during the night and through
the State of Montana and Idaho westwards.

Two things have most struck me since we crossed
the Great Divide. Up to that point we had seen no
timber of any great magnitude; and for miles and
miles through Minnesota, Dakota, and even Montana in its eastern part we had sped without seeing
any forest. Indeed the only trees visible were commonly along the rivers' banks or in their immediate
neighbourhood and accurately indicating their course.
Now, with the exception of a few places, forests are
to be seen in all directions—dense, interminable as
far as eye can reach. These forests are stately, too,
and I do feel at last that I see them as they are,
primeval. Although still at a considerable height,
the plantations frequently run right up to the very
hill-tops and against the evening sky they look at

times exceedingly picturesque standing like sentinels on guard.

Another thing. Since we crossed the Great Divide the atmosphere has not been nearly so clear as it was east. There is frequently a mugginess about it that reminded me of Liverpool and Manchester. It is said that this is caused by the great forest fires, and from what I have since seen I can quite believe it. These fires are generally intentionally begun, but get beyond control. Thus the railway for their line clearance, a settler for his land clearance, and so on, will set a forest alight, and, this done, it is not in the power of the incendiary to stop or to control it, should a period of drought and a high wind prevail. We have through miles of forest seen here and there the living fire busily engaged in its work, destroying the noblest trees and sending up volumes of thick smoke to hide and disfigure the landscape and permanently affect the atmosphere. The trees are certainly very fine, generally pine and occasionally noble cedars, and they scent the air delicately and pleasantly whether alight or not.

One other thing I have seen on the Pacific side —a clear, pebbly-beached river—Clark's Fork—by-and-by to merge in the noble Columbia River.

Through a rich country we passed rapidly during the night, and the Sunday forenoon—past Missoula, Hell's Gate (which name gave rise to a number of jokes of a more or less sulphurous character). On

and on until we came in the afternoon to Lake Pend
d'Oreille—so called, it is said, because of the district
being inhabited by Indians whose peculiarity was their
earrings. This does not seem a very satisfactory explanation of the French name.

It is a beautiful lake. Some of our party went in
the Steamer *Henry Villard*—others, including myself, preferred remaining ashore to "look up" a
Chinese settlement close by. Until we crossed the
Divide the Chinese in no way attracted our attention;
but since that crossing they are to be seen and in numbers at every stage of our journey.

Oscar Wilde, I am told, has come to the conclusion
(since American society has looked on him coldly)
that the Chinese are the only people in America who
present any fit subject for intelligent study. David
A. Wells (the celebrated leader of the Free Trade
Party in the States) thinks the future of the Chinese
nation the most important factor in the future of the
world. Putting the population of China at from 350
to 400 millions, and bearing in mind that there is not,
it is supposed, a single steam loom in the country or
indeed any of the great recent contrivances for the
economy of human labour—what, he asks, will be
the effect upon the world when this great mass of industrious humanity works with all best appliances
which human science and ingenuity can contrive? It
is an interesting problem. Meanwhile they are be-
coming· an important element in American economy.

In politics they are nil: in the labour market almost
throughout the States their influence tells.   It is certain they are industrious, frugal, temperate, and on
the whole cleanly in their personal habits.   Their
great offence in the eyes of labour is that they are
willing to work for what is considered poor pay—
or, in other words, for less than the white man will.
It is in the rudest labour principally that they now
compete, and, it follows, principally compete with
Irishmen.   With the latter consequently they are very
unpopular, and in some places where the Irish voice is
strong, as in San Francisco, the press, or portions of
it, urge legislative interference against the Chinese.
It is charged against them that they have introduced
virulent diseases previously unknown along the western coast; but the evidence of this, as I have heard the
case put, is not convincing.   One is reminded of the
charges rashly made at times in England against the
Irish labouring class and from similar motives.

Meanwhile it seems to be doubted whether to the
employer there is any real economy in Chinese labour.
General Haupt, of the Northern Pacific Railway
Company, says there is not, and I have heard his view
elsewhere confirmed.   Anyhow they have built a great
part of the Northern Pacific from the Divide to the
Pacific.   As we sped along, we came upon their encampments again and again in forest glades, by the
shores of the rivers and lakes, on the outskirts of the
cities—always a community apart.   It is to be said

to their credit that they insist, when they can, on being located near water for purposes of personal cleanliness. I am glad to see that Ward Beecher during a recent visit to San Francisco has had the courage to speak out for the Chinese against a prejudice which, although unreasoning, bids fair to be dangerous.

In the larger towns the Chinese engage in town industries, of which the favourite one with them appears to be that of laundry-men.

Mr. Wells is a remarkable and an interesting man. He is, as I said before, President of the American Free Trade League, and has through good report and evil report kept flying the Free Trade banner. He is beginning to influence his country, but the fact is the States are so prosperous, wages are so high, trade on the whole so good, capital accumulating so fast that men do not feel called upon to stop and enquire whether there is not a change which might properly be made which would quicken even that great prosperity. Mr. Wells is a regular storehouse of learning upon this question, and he found me so willing to learn from his lips that he has promised me a full copy of his Free Trade publications.

As far as I can gather, except in Pennsylvania, whose Iron Trade would be injuriously and quickly affected, there is in the United States great lethargy, and for the reasons I have given. I was, with Mr. Wells' assistance, figuring out roughly the extra cost to the Northern Pacific Railway alone over this one line from the existence of this Protection policy. It would represent a good dividend to his stockholders! Mr. Evarts in a speech he made later on (on Tuesday, in fact) said the Germans understood but could not explain the Americans and that the English explained them, but did not understand them. I wish I had had to follow him, instead of speaking as I did before him, for I would certainly have tried to make a point about the high class patriotism which reconciles the American to paying high prices for what other countries could give them cheaper and better. After all, Providence meant to give to every country a specialty or specialties for its fellows, and what cannot be got best and cheapest in one country ought to be got elsewhere. Thus is a tie of interest woven all the world over. But this smacks rather of the "Dismal Science." Finally, on Sunday night we arrived at Ainsworth, which is on the northern bank of the Snake River—tired, dusty, and perspiring, for the day was oppressive, though the pine forests through which we passed did something here and there to temper the heat.

AINSWORTH, MONDAY, SEPT. 10, 1883.

A GLORIOUS morning! Our train was drawn up close to the shining bright river, and a barge made fast near us was a good apology for a bathhouse. In we went helter-skelter to the number of

twenty or so and back again to our dining cars, and
soon our toilets completed and our appetites in better
tune for breakfast, which all the care of our host
could not prevent being somewhat monotonous. The
line of railway is incomplete at this point. The bridge
across the River Snake has not got beyond the building of the buttresses. In consequence we had to be
ferried over, and, as only about two cars at a time
could be taken, the transportation of the four trains
occupied nearly the whole day. As we were in the
second section, we started rather early, i.e., about two
o'clock—not early enough, however, to prevent the
falling night shutting out from us a perfect view of
very fine scenery.

From about Lake Pend d'Oreille we had ceased to
be in the State of Idaho, and thence until we crossed
the Snake we had been in Washington Territory (not
yet admitted to the sisterhood of the States); but,
having crossed the river, we were and continued to
be, until we reached Portland, in the large and Pacific-
bound State of Oregon.

Our course for many miles pursued pretty closely
the river; and again and again perfectly lovely
reaches of the river appeared—perfect as to colouring, volume of water, adjacent hills, trees, and the
rest. I will not stop to try to describe any one in particular.

Near a place called the Dalles there was a magnificent show of basaltic rock towering frowningly

high over our heads. There was, I assume, no real danger; but looking up from our cars we saw huge, beetling masses of rock rising, it was computed, in places to a height exceeding 100 feet and certainly looking as if falling it must fall upon us of necessity and crush us. I was not sorry when we passed it; for there was some danger, though not of the kind to which I have adverted, namely, the danger of small portions of the rock falling and being tumbled on to the line. We went slowly for caution's sake.

One beautiful scene we *did* see. It was where the river had widened out, and on either side was the wide-spreading sandy beach which tells what the Snake is in its winter fury. The warm, rich glow of the declining sun rested on everything—on the water, on the hills, on the sandy prairie, on the beach, but most of all, as it seemed, upon an encampment of the Flathead Indians which a bend in our road brought us suddenly upon. There they were as they have been since they were: no apparent tittle of change. The tepee tents, the squaws sitting about, the men lying lazily and dreamily impassive, the little ones playing, but playing noiselessly (our train was practically at a standstill) and the ponies grazing close by, except three or four, which, mounted by the chiefs, were wending their way by the riverside homeward—if the Indian has any home. To look at the picture was indeed beautiful, but I am sure if any artist could reproduce the richness of colouring it would look to the eyes of the Old World, at least to European eyes, as exaggerated and untrue to Nature.

Late in the morning of Tuesday we reached Port-land.

TUESDAY, SEPT. 11, 1883.

H ERE again we had to cross the river (here called the Willamette), but this time only the passengers and baggage. We were billetted all over the town—the arrangements certainly being as perfect as such arrangements applying to such a number can possibly be made. We elected to be billetted on board the *R. R. Thompson,* a river steamship, the property of another of Mr. Villard's successful companies called the Oregon Railway and Steam Navigation (?) Company, and here we were exceedingly comfortable during our short stay.

I will not describe Portland. It is (since we left St. Paul and Minneapolis) the most considerable town on our route by far. It is picturesquely situated on the side of a hill originally closely pine-clad and sloping down to the banks of the Willamette, which is navigable a good many miles higher. The trade of the place is considerable, and for a young city they have started and carry on in it a good many manufactures.

A great reception the town gave—gay in banners with hospitable legends upon them, gay in triumphal arches, gay in flowers, and perhaps above all, gay in the bright looks and holiday dresses of its people. A great procession took place from the landing stage to the large pavilion or public room of the town—a procession intended to represent the early history and the present state of the city headed by the early pioneers or their descendants and concluding with exhibits of the now various trades and manufactures of its people.

I arrived at the pavilion late and found that some of the English guests were expected to speak and that Horace Davey was asked to do so. He was anxious that I should take his place, and I, while by no means eager to deprive him of the honour, was unwilling to seem to decline a responsibility which my seniority as a silkgown seemed to put upon me. Eventually we both spoke.

Mr. George, Senator for the State of Oregon, delivered to Mr. Villard the congratulatory address. Mr. George was what the Americans call "the orator of the day." He is a young, good-looking man of colossal height and brown hair. He is not so gross and fat as Gambetta was, but he nevertheless reminded me of the dead Frenchman. But not in his oratory. He read a carefully prepared essay, sensible and clever enough, but he endeavoured by violence of gesture and stress of voice to give it the effect of spoken speech, and failed therein. Mr. Villard in response, speaking apparently impromptu, spoke sensibly and well.

CARL SCHURZ

He then called upon me. My friends said I did very well; but they were friends. For my own part I felt when I had sat down that I had several things to say worth listening to, and I could not recollect anything I had uttered of which this could truly be said. Two men spoke later whom I was for different reasons glad to hear. One Mr. Carl Schurz because I had never heard him before, and the other Evarts, because, having heard him on this occasion, I was able to understand how he had acquired the high reputation he possessed.

Carl Schurz was Minister of the Interior under a former government and was remarkable for his wise and conciliatory policy towards the Indians, in whose regard he had established schools for the education of their young. He said (on Tuesday) amongst many other wise and statesmanlike things that public men now saw that it was not only wiser and more generous but cheaper to conciliate and to educate than to fight and trample upon the Indians. He is a German, but he speaks English more correctly than any foreigner I have ever heard, and more correctly than any American speaker, according at least to our English ideas.

Evarts, of Tuesday, was not the Evarts who heavily delivered a heavy oration at Spike Point on last Saturday. That Evarts was prosy, indulging in long and complicated sentences difficult to parse, labouring to be impressive and I fear ending only in being dull:

this Evarts spoke as if he had no weight on his mind: his sentences were terse and pointed. He was at will humorous or satirical, and once or twice by impromptu hints carried his audience entirely with him. I was delighted with his speech, and greatly pleased that I had not to leave America with my first impressions of his powers unremoved.

Generally those I have heard here show very considerable speech-ability. The audiences, too, seem to enjoy the oratory. It is in voice and gesture more vigourous than in England is usual; and certainly there is a boldness (not to say exaggeration) of metaphor which we should think overstrained if not grotesque, but which here finds pleased acceptance.

In the evening was a grand concert followed by a reception and in full dress! We donned our best, and as in duty bound paid our respects to Mr. Villard. We left early, for to-morrow (Wednesday) we detach ourselves from the main body of the party and go in advance at 5 A.M. via Kalama, Tacoma, Puget Sound, Seattle, and across the Straits of Juan de Fuca to Victoria in Vancouver Island—where we again touch Great British Dominion.

The assembly was sufficiently brilliant and distinguished. Of the music I cannot speak highly, but in such matters it is not fair to be critical in a new city of a new country. One is astonished not at what is not but at what is.

As Dr. Gneist said to me on Tuesday, they still have a good deal to learn from the Old World, though they do not know it nor how much they already owe it.

WEDNESDAY, SEPT. 12, 1883.

STARTING at 5 A.M. by the good S. S. *Dixie Thompson* we proceed to Kalama, sailing down the Willamette and barely touching the Columbia, on the whole the noblest river I have yet seen here. I am told that further south the Mississippi and Missouri will open my eyes.

We ought to have breakfasted on board, but two hungry hordes of passengers descended with such swiftness and determination upon the breakfast that there was nothing for us. At Kalama at 12 o'clock we made a modest meal and pursued our journey by train to Tacoma, the city of the most southerly part of Puget Sound.

There is nothing in the country between Kalama and Tacoma to call for special mention. The country is low-lying and in parts very swampy. The forests are dense and the timber of very large size, while the luxuriance of vegetation shows that the yearly rainfall must be very considerable. One resident said with a grin: "No man that ain't web-footed need come here." Again and again along the route we were struck with the devastation the forest fires have wrought. For miles here and there, the noblest trees

literally in thousands upon thousands burnt to char-
coal, and whole acres of underwood and its accompanying vegetation burnt to the ground. I am beginning to realise (what must be accepted as an un-
doubted fact) that the smoke from these fires for
weeks and for months troubles the air and obscures
the landscape.

We had a special grudge against the fires to-day.
Some sixty miles from Tacoma, but well in view from
its neighbourhood, is the mighty perpetually snow-clad
mountain Rainier, some 14,440 feet high. It is also
sometimes called Mount Tacoma.

I must break off here, suddenly and unexpectedly.
We have got so far as Tacoma on our way back to
Portland to-day (Saturday), intending to sail by the
S. S. *Columbia* from Portland this evening for San
Francisco.

Here, however, we are overtaken by the *Queen of
the Pacific* bound for San Francisco—a splendid vessel with lots of room; and, as we are kindly offered
the option of going by her, we gladly accept it. I
have a magnificent stateroom—so large that even on
land it would hardly seem mean. It is luxuriously furnished. Furthermore this change saves a journey
back to Portland of about 200 miles or so, and se-
cures for us what I was anxious for, namely, the sail
down and not merely across the Juan de Fuca Straits.
I write on Saturday, Sept. 15, 1883, at Tacoma on
board the S. S. *Queen of the South* (? Pacific).

TACOMA, WASHINGTON.   VIEW FROM NEW COURT-HOUSE

WEDNESDAY, SEPT. 12, 1883 (*cont'd*).

I BROKE off as we approached Tacoma. Rainier, eagerly looked for by many in our train, declined to show himself. I was amused at the personal interest taken in him by the Tacomians and the eagerness they showed that we should get a satisfactory view. Later, when I saw the mountain myself, I ceased to be surprised.

We had a few hours to spare at Tacoma, and walked through the old and new towns—that is, through the town a few years and the town a few months old. The situation is very fine. Beginning at the base of a bold bluff originally clothed in pine, the towns rise up the slopes to the plateau above; and still further back hills rise again forming a beautiful background. This is the beginning of Puget Sound, remarkable for its astounding water depths. It is a novel complaint, but it is literally the complaint here at Tacoma, that there is too much water—so much indeed as to interfere with anchorage facilities. One hundred yards from the shore there are 100 fathoms or more of depth!

From this point past Juan de Fuca Straits to George's Bay is here sometimes called the Mediterranean of the West. It is certainly very beautiful. Hence to Victoria we do not lose sight (save in a fog) of land, and wherever we sight it we see bluffs of greater or less height, but all densely covered with noble pine forests from top to water's edge.

The principal trade of Tacoma, as also of Seattle, Port Madison, Port Ludlow, Port Gamble, and Port Townsend, where our steamer touches, is the lumber trade. In each of these places there is one or more saw-mills busily engaged in the trade. At Tacoma there is also a coal trade. The Union Pacific Railway Company find it suits their purpose to buy a coal mine in this neighbourhood, make a railroad and expensive coal chute in connection with it, and keep a fleet of ships trading to and from San Francisco for the supply of their engines! The mine is at Carbonado. We sailed at night in the S. S. *North Pacific,* and so saw little of the Sound on our out voyage, until close to the Island of San Juan we sighted the noble range of mountains to the west called Olympian in Washington Territory. The sovereignty of this Island (San Juan) was, you will recollect, some years ago in dispute between England and America, but by the arbitrament of the Emperor of Germany was awarded to America. The question seems to have turned upon the point whether the Island was upon the American or upon the Vancouver Island side of the main channel.

Speedily, about 12 o'clock Thursday morning, we sight Vancouver Island.

VICTORIA, VANCOUVER ISLAND, THURSDAY,
SEPT. 13, 1883.

THE island is pleasant but not of striking aspect, as we near the narrow, very narrow, approach to the harbour of Victoria. The coast is rockbound, like a great part of the Irish and Scotch coasts; and inland it seems diversified by hill and valley without any considerable amount of agricultural land in any one district. It seems, too, generally well and heavily timbered, and has valuable and extensive coal mines. The climate during our short stay was delicious. It was an English autumn fine day with a clear sky and a bright sun, pleasantly warm and yet with a dash of winter in the air. The inhabitants say it is fine weather eight months in the year.

Victoria has certainly not the go-ahead look of the new American towns. Comparatively, things were staid and dull, though there were signs of solid business in the place. Sites for building certainly run high. My barber, who charged me half a dollar, equal to 2s. English money, told me he paid $2 per foot per month frontage for a frontage of twenty-five feet and that he then had to build his house, covenanting to leave it at the end of his term on the land. This would be a ground rent of £120 a year.

Accompanied by one of the Hudson Bay Company's officials (Mr. Munro) we had a very pleasant drive from Victoria, past Esquimalt (pronounce Squimalt) towards Goldstream.

Squimalt is a small, very small town, but the harbour is greatly superior to Victoria. Indeed if there is ever any considerable town at this end of the island, it must, I think, be at Squimalt and not at Victoria. A good many people with whom I have talked agreed in this and think a mistake has been made by the Canadian Pacific Company, who propose Port Moody on the Georgian Bay as the terminus of their trans-continental line. It is argued that they ought to have gone further north (where it is said the climate is at least as temperate) and crossing the narrows between the mainland and Vancouver's Island continue their railway system right down to Squimalt Bay. This would give to the Canadian Pacific Company that important desideratum, a good port closer to the Pacific than any United States line in the Northwest can boast of. It is also further objected that Port Moody is not itself a good harbour and that the approaches to it are difficult of navigation. Besides all this it is agreed it would have enabled the Canadian line to tap a fertile district of Canada further north.

The formation of a railroad is now in contemplation from Navarino in the north of the Island to a point somewhere close to Victoria.

There is good coal in the north, and there is some gold, but nothing of any moment.

The British ship *Swiftsure* (man-of-war) lay in

Squimalt, and I regret to say in the course of our drive we saw more drunken men, all from this ship, than I have so far seen in all my trip in the United States.

FRIDAY, SEPT. 14, 1883.
(*En route* back from Victoria to Tacoma.)

WE slept on board our good ship *The North Pacific* and 5.15 A.M. found us well under way. A couple of buckets of salt water soon thoroughly roused us to the signal beauty of the morning and the scene. By the way, the water in the Straits and in Puget Sound is very cold—so cold indeed that except in the very height of summer it is very little used for bathing and then only by venturous hot-blooded youth. The people call it "snow-water," and at first I found it difficult to understand that this was anything more than a quaint conceit or popular exaggeration. But to-day I saw there were (as there generally are for all popular beliefs) solid grounds for this view. On the one side of the Sound to the west as we sail for Seattle and Tacoma is the great range known as the Olympian. It is the westerly and northerly boundary of Washington Territory; and, although not to be compared with other mountains of greater height, it covers a large extent of country.

On the east is another range of mountains, and close to the American and Canadian dividing line is Mount Baker, the noblest mountain I ever saw, ex-

cept Rainier, otherwise called Tacoma. I did not see
Mount Baker till Saturday evening, but I saw Rainier
on the Friday evening. The day was much brighter,
and the atmosphere much clearer as we approached
Seattle on our return. I had my glasses and was suddenly attracted by what seemed a bright cloud resting
on a darker one close to the horizon line. It had,
however, a fixity about it that puzzled me, when a
voice at my elbow said: "Well, Sir, and what do you
think of our little hill? I guess it's as big as some
mountains in your country." This, then, was Rainier.
As I look upon it, I confess to myself it is the grand-
est creation I ever saw. It is 14,440 feet above ocean
level. The lower part about two-thirds up is pine-
clad (I had mistaken it for a darker coloured cloud),
but the remaining one-third is covered (as I look upon
it, as it is perpetually) with snow. We were very
lucky to see it, for it is often months that Royal
Rainier hides himself.

As we approach Seattle (still on our way back
to Tacoma) all things warn us that Seattle is
en fête.

The steamboats and the sailing boats, big and little, all sport their available bunting; and, as we come
close to the landing wharf, we see triumphal arches
prepared for the great Villard, who following us
from Victoria, is presently to arrive. Here we were
obliged to change boats; and, having left the party
at Portland, we judged it best to keep to ourselves.

MT. RAINIER AND REFLECTION LAKE,
RAINIER NATIONAL PARK

But it was fated that we should rejoin it at Tacoma, and under circumstances to us particularly agreeable.

We went up the hill on which Seattle is built, and from that vantage ground witnessed the procession of vessels which went down the Strait to do honour to Villard. It was in every way a pleasant sight, picturesque to the eye and suggestive, too. I won't describe Seattle beyond saying it is bigger and more advanced than Tacoma.

Between Seattle, Tacoma, and Port Townsend (a smaller place than either, situate nearer the Fuca Straits and on the west of Puget Sound) rivalry now exists. Each place asserts itself as the only place where the N. P. Railway Company can find a proper and commodious outlet to the Pacific seas.

By the time we sailed for Tacoma, the day was declining, and the illumination of Seattle was at its best, as we rounded the point close by, which shut out our view. It was a lovely night, and I must say I never had so perfect a view of any illumination, and I never saw any which to my eye looked half as well. Built on the side of a hill, the town rose terrace above terrace, and from the *Queen of the Pacific* (the steamship which carried the excursion party) to the public-school—a fine building which crowns the city—all was ablaze.

At Tacoma, which we reached about 11 o'clock (passed on our way by the speedier *Queen of the South*), we experienced what appeared to be a stroke of ill luck. The only hotel would not have us: it was full. If it had not been full, we should both have tumbled into bed, and next morning journeyed on above 150 miles to Portland in order to sail thence on Saturday night by the S. S. *Columbia* for San Francisco. As it was, I walked down to the wharf alongside which lay the *Queen*. I met my good friend Mr. Garrison, whose unobtrusive kindness I shall not readily forget. He informed me that not only could we get accommodation on board, but that, if it suited us equally well, we could sail in the *Queen* direct for San Francisco instead of making the weary journey (retracing one's steps is always weary) back to Portland. We were delighted, and all difficulty as to Darling (whom we left in Portland) and our baggage there being promptly overcome by telegram, we gratefully turned in to our new quarters—and what quarters! The *Queen* is a very fine and a very fast ship; and it is no exaggeration to say that expense and ingenuity have not been spared in making her the most luxurious boat I ever saw. My apartment is splendid. I should be content to go in the *Queen* round even by Cape Horn and so home to England.

I found General Grant had left the party at Portland, returning to New York with Mr. Billings, Mr. Evarts and Mr. Grant, his son. I think I have already said that General Grant is the *one* man who is generally popular in the United States. It was a pleasant sight to see the old veterans who had served under him, but who have since "turned their swords into ploughshares," clustering round the car (which was next ours) to have a word and a grasp of the hand from him. There was no ceremony about the matter. Any one who wanted to talk with him walked into the car and was always well received. There was something refreshing in all this absence of those class distinctions which with us exist. Here was a man who twice filled the highest executive post under the Constitution, accessible to all from high to low. I could not help thinking of those royal journeys so carefully ordered that the vulgar gaze of the people could not even penetrate to the stations along the line.

SATURDAY, SEPT. 15, 1883.
(*En route* Tacoma in Puget Sound to San Francisco.)

THIS was a most delightful day, but wholly uneventful. The great body of our party left by 7 o'clock train for Portland, intending to return to New York by the route already traversed, but making a stay of four days at Yellowstone Park in order to explore the glories of that wonderful district.

As the train left the depot, the stern whistle of the *Queen* sounded, and soon we were speeding at 15 knots (or nearly) the hour down the Sound for Port Townsend, which was our clearance port. Nothing could possibly be more agreeable than the day. The clouds had nearly all lifted; the atmosphere was

brilliant; the sun warm and bright, and we were thus
enabled to see under the most favourable conditions
the beauties of the Mediterranean of the northwest.

Take it all in all, the finest view I have yet seen
was that which lay around us after we had cleared
Port Townsend and were standing in a westerly direction down the Juan de Fuca Straits for the great
Pacific Ocean. The weather I have already described. To the north lay the island of San Juan,
and then a little to the northwest Vancouver Island
—pleasant objects for the eye to rest upon, but not
of commanding beauty. To the south (the southern
boundary of the Straits as Vancouver Island is the
northern) the fine Olympian range, in never-melting
snow atop and at bottom fringed by a dense fringe of
pine and cedar forest. Here and there great clouds
of freshly risen smoke showed us that the forest fires
were at work, but the wind was from the northwest
and pretty strong, and these did not obscure our view.
The waters of the Sound are now quickly shut out
from us, for Washington Territory and the State of
Oregon appear to join hands; and here right astern of
us to the east is the great picture of the scene, the
noble Mount Baker nearly 13,000 feet high and
seeming all the bigger from his superiority over his
smaller brethren who are not far off. As we go down
the strait farther and farther to the west, and farther
and farther from Mount Baker, I find it impossible
to withdraw my eyes from it: it seems to exert a kind

of fascination over me, and certainly, as we recede, it seems to tower more and more into the sky until the intervening pine-clad bluffs have disappeared; and it stands noble and alone lifting its mighty head high up from the horizon line! At last we lose it in the gradual coming shadows of night. I saw it better and for a longer time than Rainier, but men who know both well say Rainier is the grander mountain, as it is certainly the higher by between 1,000 and 2,000 feet.

On we go, down the Sound, past the lighthouses which north and south—on English and American territory respectively—mark the entrance from the Straits into the great Pacific. The beauty of the night tempts many of us to remain on deck far into the night; and, giving the mainland a wide berth, we rapidly run south, round Cape Flattery, past Destruction Island, past Gray's Harbour (called after the Captain Gray who first discovered the mouths of the Columbia River) past Cape Disappointment and the Columbia mouths. At last I go to my very roomy and luxurious quarters, pleasantly tired but not exhausted, and at peace with all the world.

·

SUNDAY, SEPT. 16, 1883.
(2nd day. *En route* from Tacoma to San Francisco.)

AGAIN a delightful but uneventful day! The Pacific is still true to its name, but it is a mistake to suppose that there is not frequently along the coast very heavy weather. Our captain (Alexander) tells me this is altogether about the best trip he has ever had along the coast. Going north he says they had nothing but fog and smoke with lumpy seas—this time almost a smooth sea, and there has not been a moment we have lost sight of land.

It is a remarkable fact that from Port Townsend in Puget Sound on the north, to the port San Tego in the south, there is not a single harbour which a stranger in distress can safely enter except San Francisco. This is a distance of some 1,200 miles in extent!

Speaking of our captain reminds me that the three first officers on board this fine vessel, i.e., the captain and the first mate and second mate, are all remarkably young men. The captain does not look to be more than forty years, if so much, while the first and second mates are under thirty. Promotion in the merchant service here seems to be quicker than with us.

The line of the Pacific coast, as we now view it, is disappointing. There are comparatively no big coast bluffs or mountains. The coast is generally rockbound, with a low line of hills lying a little inland, and these are, as a rule, covered with forests. Beyond there is a fertile valley and then still farther inland (but not visible to us) is a further range of grander mountains called in Oregon State the Cascade Range, and, where it reappears farther south in the State of California, called the Sierra Nevada

Range. The really fertile lands lie principally to the west of these and in the valleys.

Mr. Tully, a member of Congress, returned by a district of the State of California, whose acquaintance I have here had the pleasure of making, tells me that good weather for harvesting is such a certainty that the farmers leave their threshed grain in the open fields until it is convenient to cart it away to the depots. I wish Ireland could count upon such a harvest-time as this!

I find Mr. Tully is a sound and well-informed Free Trader. We had quite a lively discussion this morning to give us an appetite for breakfast. Ex-Governor Perkins of the State of California and Mr. Davis, ex-Congressman, took the Protection side and Mr. Tully (firing an effective shot now and then) left to me the main brunt of the fighting. As he afterwards phrased it, "I guess I thought I could leave you to do the chewing up."

I am not going to go into this question here, but I must say that while I've discussed it with many able and generally well-informed men, from Mr. Evarts to ex-Governor Perkins, not one of them has really argued or even attempted to argue the question. They seem to think they have said all that was necessary and proved the whole case by exclaiming, "Sir, under the Protective system you condemn we've built up the prosperous cities and communities you've witnessed." It is no use to answer that this is a very bad example of the *post hoc propter hoc* argument, and that I might with just as much force reply, "Yes, in spite of Protection you certainly have some prosperity." Neither does it matter to these logicians to point out that the inventors of their Tariff system, the Hamiltons and the Clays, expressly advocated it as only a temporary expedient to help an infant commerce to get over the ills and weaknesses of infancy. One thing, however, struck me very forcibly. The dislike of England is deep down in the breast of Americans—at least of Americans of the North. Senators and Congressmen alike have dropped remarks strongly indicative of this. They still feel sorely the privateer proceedings in which some English firms took a prominent part in their war crisis, and they add with some bitterness, "But we made England pay for it." One thing is clear that any advocacy by England of Free Trade doctrines will retard, not advance the question.

Another thing strikes me strongly. In the American press throughout the entire extent of country I have travelled I have noticed that the so-called English news is almost entirely confined to news relating to Irish questions—the National movement, Irish land, and so forth. All this has its strong significance.

We are still discussing Free Trade and American interests in relation thereto (it has broken out afresh) as the sun goes down behind a curtain of bright gold,

giving promise that the delightful weather we have
had will be with us to the end. To-morrow (Monday) night we hope with continued good luck to
reach the Golden Gates which lead to San Francisco.

MONDAY, SEPT. 17, 1883.
(Still (3d day) *en route* from Tacoma to San
Francisco.)

ONCE more a delightful but uneventful day! Unless indeed the fact that in the bright sunlight
since morning mighty whales have been disporting
themselves ahead of and all round us in great numbers can be called an event. I am sure Bertie would
consider it so. Well, Bertie, I will tell you all I know
about them. "There's a whale, good for forty bar-
rels at least," cries the second officer, and, looking
where he points, I see a disturbance of the otherwise
unruffled surface of the water—nothing more. Presently a little way off up goes a great waterspout thus:
. . . and the officer shouts out "there's another."
This time I see clearly enough a black object, bigger
than any live object I ever before saw in the sea,
floating for a moment or two lazily on the surface and
then he disappears.

These appearances, Bertie, you will understand,
occurred again and again through the day; but I saw
no more than I saw at my first introduction to a whale.
In fact, these big creatures, Bertie, do not display

their immensity on the surface; they only come up from time to time, displaying a black fin on the top of their back and disappearing.

As we got farther south, the outlines of the shore were bolder, the bluffs higher and occasionally very fine—reminding me greatly of Ireland—say the coast of Antrim, but nothing, I think, like so fine as parts of the Antrim coast.

As we were finishing dinner (I enclose bill of fare, which was a real Bill, for Frank's delectation) our courteous Captain, rising from the table, said: "Gentlemen, I hope you will come on deck a few minutes, for we shall soon be passing through the 'Golden Gate.'"

Presently up we went. We were approaching the entrance to this, the finest harbour I ever saw. On each side were lighthouses and also strong fortifications for the defence of the Port, and a little farther to the south was a great rock known as Seal Rock, on which literally thousands of seals hourly and daily disport themselves. On, on we go, and now, fairly through the entrance, we see the straggling lights of this the greatest city of the South. But the Golden Gate —where is it? Why so called? I look eagerly forward, but all I see in the dull light of the rapidly closing day is a murky smoky atmosphere such as one sees in the busy towns of Lancashire. Why the Golden Gate? In my perplexity I turn back to the west which we are leaving, and I need no further ex-

planation. The revelation is made to me. The sun
has gone down but left the traces of his bright golden
glory behind him, and there between the two head-
lands which form the pillars (themselves gilt by the
brightness all around them) we see only one blaze of
rich golden light from side to side. It is well called
the Golden Gate. A turn in our course presently
shuts out this brightness from our view, and we discern in the dull light a number of vessels anchored in
what seems and is, in fact, an immense anchorage
ground. We tread our way cautiously amongst them,
and, finally landed at Broadway Wharf, we are taken
possession of by the employees of the Palace Hotel,
San Francisco, and within its hospitable portals we
speedily find ourselves. I will by-and-by tell you
what San Francisco is like.

TUESDAY, SEPT. 18, 1883.

My impressions of yesterday evening of the
beauty of this place were quite confirmed this
morning. We arrived at the Palace Hotel and found
it all ablaze and a band playing in the atrium (Arthur
will explain) or court-yard, which was crowded.

Our rooms had been engaged and were the best in
the house—on the sixth story! They were really very
fine—large, lofty, with bathroom and dressing-room
to each—in fact, very complete suites of rooms. In
the morning we found we had a distant view of the

bay and across to Goat Island over the intervening city.

'Frisco is certainly beautifully situated and beautifully laid out. Sheltered from the west by the southern arm of the bay, it rests upon a succession of hills —many of them very steep—which seem to run almost in regular parallel lines.

Though much smaller in population than Chicago, it is a much more taking city. There is also great appearance of business activity. Altogether, after New York it is the finest city I have seen here.

The system of tramcars is the most perfect I have seen. Even the steepest hills are charged by steam-trams worked on the endless-chain principle, and you can travel from one end of the city to the other for five cents. This is the only cheap thing, this tram travelling, which I have yet come across in the United States.

I went early to St. Mary's Hospital, situated on the top of Rincon Hill. I was being shown into a parlour when Kate appeared—looking on the whole very well and strong, and exactly as she looked when in Great Britain four years ago—not looking a day older.

The Sisters of Mercy were not the first religious Sisterhood in 'Frisco, but they have since their arrival, about 1854, made marked progress. Outside the convent and outside the Catholic community the noble work they have done is gratefully acknowledged.

On Rincon Hill they have a large Hospital, a work-school, and a Home for aged women.

They have altogether five branches in 'Frisco, and in Sacramento, and have in charge several schools. They receive no aid from the State, and no compensation for the important teaching services which they render. Neither do any others of the Catholic Schools. In this important particular Catholic schools are much better off in England.

Kate inquired very anxiously about everybody at home, and I gave her the fullest particulars I could. She complains that, although they have been promised to her, she has not received the photos of Margaret, Lily, May, and Bertie. This should be seen to. I am sure also she would like photos of little Willie and Alice.

I also saw Mary Martin in her nun's dress. (She used to be a companion of my mother.) She is a bright, cheery little nun.

Joseph Jennings is here, carrying on the business of an Insurance Agent under the firm of Jennings & Stillman. He has very good offices in a good business street and seems to be doing a good business. Kate speaks in the highest terms of him and of his family. The latter live in Chicago. I thought Joseph Jennings looking old and thin, but I believe I look nearly as old myself, although I am a good many years his junior. He speaks with great regard of Kate.

It appears that, when following his profession of

engineer a good many years ago, his left eye became affected and continues to be so. But otherwise his sight is good. I also saw James Gartlan, whom I could not recollect ever having seen in Ireland. I easily recognised him for his likeness to his brother George, B.L., in Dublin. He seems very well and in good spirits. He is working very hard for the Law, which here covers a great deal of ground—including the parts of Barrister and of Attorney, and also a wide field of business-work besides.

Tell Letitia Jennings in Newry and Alexander Gartlan about their respective relatives.

WEDNESDAY, SEPT. 19, 1883.

WE drove out this morning at 6.30 to Cliff House, situated about eight miles from 'Frisco and opposite the famous Seal Rocks (to which I have before alluded) for breakfast. We went through the Park, which is of great extent and beautifully laid out, and here I travelled on the first good road which I've seen in the United States. The roads in town and country are, generally speaking, simply execrable.

The Rocks are certainly remarkable. They are literally covered with seals, and the water about them seems literally swimming with them. They seem to be on the best terms with the wild birds, with whom they share possession in a quite friendly way.

The hotel has a name for breakfast, and accord-

ingly we ordered what proved a very expensive one,
and a very bad one and included in our menu one of
the American delicacies, viz.: terrapin. Terrapin is
a kind of small land turtle. Well, this is the third
great American delicacy that has deceived me. The
other two are sweet corn and soft-shell crab. But I
wish to say that I do not think I ate any one of them
under favourable conditions. The fact is you require
to be introduced to these delicacies under extremely
favourable auspices, or you may possibly do them a
life-long injustice! I should like to avoid this.

A great friend of Kate's, a Mr. Oliver, called upon
me, accompanied by his son-in-law, Mr. Tobin, who
is a banker and practising lawyer in this place. Mr.
Oliver and Mr. Tobin are Irishmen, and the former
is one of the many men here who are reputed millionaires.

We had with both a good deal of conversation
about Ireland and Irishmen at home and abroad.
They are both, I should say, strong Parnellites in the
main. Mr. Tobin commands a volunteer local regi-
ment and he has under him men of '48 and 1866, and
even one man who took part in the Tallaght episode
on the borders of Dublin and Wicklow, only a few
years ago. The Irishmen here are strongly national,
as indeed they generally are throughout the United
States.

As to the position of Irishmen in 'Frisco, it is good,
very good. A native American told me he considered

their rise remarkable, bearing in mind the fact that they come to this country the worst provided to battle successfully in their new life in the three important points of education, skilled training, and money.

Since 1863 there has been no serious collapse in trade; but in that year the town was in an awful state for want of employment for the poor. Kate told me that in that time they fed at the convent daily some 300 persons. Here the Chinese question presents the gravest difficulty. The Chinese number in this city about 60,000. There is more complexity in this matter than I at first thought. It is objected that these Chinese, unlike the German, Irish, and other like classes of emigrants, do not come here intending to form any part personally of the body politic. They do not coalesce with the other classes. They stand apart; they are neither given nor give in marriage, and their savings, instead of going to increase the national wealth, are steadily hoarded to be spent by them (after a few years' sojourn here) in their native land. It is objected that it is unfair to bring the labour of such a class as this into competition with and to the prejudice of the classes who are part of the country and who are willing, if necessary, to fight for it.

It seems on all hands admitted that, although Chinese honesty does not stand high, Chinese industry, intelligence, and ingenuity do. The Chinese have a theatre here.

[I wish here to note (out of place) that Kate objects to the American Free School System on one ground, which Cardinal Manning takes against the English School Board System. It is this: that it pauperises education, that it enables persons who are fully able to pay or at least to contribute to the education of their children to come *in formâ pauperis* to the Free Schools.]

We visited a remarkable yearly exhibition of the manufactures of the State of California at the Mechanics' Institute. It certainly gives a wide idea of the development of their local manufactures and of the wealth of the locality. Their furniture was particularly rich and luxurious in design. They have got in this State on the coast a red wood (unknown elsewhere) which is soft and easily worked and which takes a polish as fine as mahogany. This wood, I see, enters largely into their furniture-making.

We left in the evening *via* the Ferry and Oakland for Madera, about 180 miles from 'Frisco *en route* for the far-famed Yosemite.

Our line followed the inland portion of this great Bay for many miles, and passing through a great wheat-bearing country, namely the valley of the San Roque, we finally arrived at Madera at 11.45, intending to pass the night in the Pullman cars.

It was remarkable the enormous number of sacks of grain which we found piled up in the open air unprotected, on the ground or in open wagons *en route* for shipment at San Francisco. The faith of the

farmers in the dryness of the weather is great, and
appears to be well founded. It is now just a month
since I landed at New York and I affirm that during
the whole of that term I have not noticed altogether
one hour's rain! When in the Northwest, it was said
there was some rain one night, but I do not vouch for
the fact. This dryness has its inconvenience, as my
next day's chronicle will attest, but to the farmer who
wants his grain saved these inconveniences count for
little.

THURSDAY, SEPT. 20, 1883.

IF ON the evening of Thursday, September 20th,
I had wanted to punish my direst enemy with
severity, I would have enjoined his riding by the
American stage from Madera to Clark (a distance
of about seventy miles) in the tail seat on a hot day!
We started at 6 o'clock sharp and were journeying in
pain and misery until close upon 8 o'clock in the evening, altogether fourteen hours! Whence the trouble,
you will ask? Answer, everywhere. The carriage
had no springs, and the driver drove as if it had. The
road was full of boulder stones and ruts, and the
driver drove his team as if he were tooling round
Hyde Park. Bump, bump, every two or three minutes; you are shot up in the air a foot or so, be the
same more or less, and come down on the hard seat
in a manner to seriously affect, temporarily at least,
the base of the spine. Nor was this all. The dust

lay feet deep in the ground (they have had no rain since April) and as the six horses galloped along, we at the end were enveloped in clouds of dust so thick at times that we could not see the horses in front. Anything like the suffocating feeling I never before experienced, for, be it remembered, the thermometer was at 98° in the shade! At last we got to the end of the weariest day's journey I ever made. I made a rush for the bathroom, and having secured primary possession I left after a few minutes, intimate with soap, water, and scrubbers, so that I became again recognisable by my friends. The sight of all the passengers was bad, but Martin and I were the worst. I am sure I had enough dust down my back to furnish a moderate-sized dust-bin!

I can now look back with more equanimity on the proceedings of the morning. For the early part of the day we passed through a flat, uninteresting country which, however, is said to be great at wheat-bearing, but was to-day bare and parched. We passed several beds of rivers where obviously in winter and spring the water brawls loudly, and found nothing but dry sand and boulders. Indeed until we reached a village called Fresno Flats, I did not see a single running stream, although we passed many dry beds.

. One curious and interesting thing we noticed. Close by our trail or road ran for miles a kind of trough supported by timber at heights from the

ground.   Now and then we lost sight of it for hours,
but again it reappeared.   I thought it must be some
irrigation apparatus (and probably it helped irrigation also), but that is not its main purpose.   It is a
timber chute, some fifty miles long!   The timber is
cut in the mountain fifty miles up country and sent
down baulk by baulk by means of water, which in
spring is plentiful enough.   This will give you a good
idea of the vastness of the country, and how little its
people reckon about distances.   Fancy such a thing in
Ireland stretching from Dublin to Newry!

By-and-by we gain the forest land, and bit by bit
make our way up the approaches to the Sierra Nevada
Range, in which lies the wondrous Yosemite Valley.
The forest-road track is startling in the extreme.   It
is not wider in any place than about twenty feet, and
it winds in and out and in and out of the mountain
gorges and along very precipitous hills, margined
more frequently than not by a steep fall many feet
deep.   I am not nervous, but I confess I did not at all
like our road.   But our driver, not coachman (I committed a great offence by so calling him), rattled his
six horses along round the sharp turns with great skill
and also great unconcern.   Occasionally looking back
the track we made seemed uncomfortably close to the
edge.   Later still our difficulty was greater, for we
were overtaken by the night, and yet on we went as if
it were all plain sailing, and finally arrived at Clark's
on the slope of a hill about 3,000 feet above sea level,

but still about twenty-five difficult miles from the Yosemite.

Clark's was a fairly comfortable hostelry, and, like all the hotels that we have visited west, was serupulously clean.

A simple meal, and I was soon between the sheets and speedily forgetful of an unpleasant day's drive.

FRIDAY, SEPT. 21, 1883.

I NOTE here lest I should forget and because I know Mrs. Macaulay will be interested in the fact that Joshua O'Neill, formerly in Mr. Macaulay's employment at Randalstown, is now bookkeeper or clerk at the Hibernian Bank, San Francisco. I have not yet seen him, but I intend to try to do so on my return.

This day our drive was continued through mountainous forests just like the latter part of yesterday's drive. The timber was magnificent. It was quite common to see trees bordering the road five and six and even eight feet in diameter and 250 feet and upwards in height and straight as a lance. Indeed the timber was quite as fine in the forest approaches as in the valley itself.

We started at 7 o'clock and were due at Cook's in the valley at 2 o'clock. At about 12.30 we were laboriously surmounting the last mountain spur which lies between us and the valley, and about 1 o'clock a glorious view certainly burst upon us. We were at Inspiration Point! From a height of still several hundred feet above the valley, which is itself about 4,000 feet above the sea, we are looking down upon the greatest aggregate of noble mountains I ever before saw at one moment.

Close to us to the left is Il Capitan, a rock of several thousand feet, which rises sheer up from the valley. To our right is also the Bridal Veil Fall (900 feet unbroken fall), in which the volume of water is just now small, but which even now is suggestive of its name from the lace-like appearance the water presents as the wind catches and seems to spread it out in its long descent. Also to our right is Sentinel Dome, rising abruptly from the valley and from which we afterwards got our best view, or at all events our second best. Further on to the left was Glacier Point, a rock rising perpendicularly from the valley with an unbroken continuous face exceeding 3,000 feet! And still further away were, faintly appearing in the distance, the peaks and points of the Lyall and Obelisk groups of mountains—the former some 13,000 feet in height. On our left was Eagle's Point and Cloud's Rest—the latter some 10,000 feet high. All the mountains bounding the valley are granite, and at first sight present the appearance of being snow-clad; but, in fact, patches and small patches only of snow now rest upon them. The valley is rich in land and in timber, and the hardy pine clings to what seems the clayless rocks and is to be found rearing its head high up the sides, and even on the very tops of the highest mountains.

I have just re-read what I have written, and I see I have failed to emphasise sufficiently the characteristic look of the valley, which is that the rock mountains, like walls, rise perpendicularly all round it; and indeed the very faces of the rocks are smooth and polished. In fact, the idea which was forced upon my mind was that the bottom has fallen out here and left the walls standing. I find that my unlettered view is accepted by some savant called Whitney, who says the existing state could only have been produced by volcanic action involving enormous subsidence. Others refer to the glacier theory as explaining it. It appears this valley is, after all, known to the white man only some thirty years. About that time the Indians were making very successful cattle raids, and it could not be discovered whither the cattle were driven. At last an expedition, headed by a Captain Boling, succeeded in discovering the valley and a large party of Indians with great numbers of cattle. After considerable fighting these Indians were driven out of the valley, and escaped by what is called to this day the Indians' Cañon, which looked at to-day with our eyes seems impenetrable and impassable.

Opinions differed in our party of ten as to the grandeur of the scene, but on the whole opinion seemed to be that, while this was the more peculiar and remarkable view, some of the Swiss views are grander. We will, I hope, Madam, next year see some of these grand Swiss views together.

Cook's Hotel in the valley is an aggregation of small wooden huts. Nearly all are one story high; but it was cleanly and comfortable, and the food excellent.

We were to be up betimes in the morning to see the sun rise *in* Mirror Lake, and so we were off early to bed. What this mystery means, the sun rising *in* the Lake, will hereafter appear.

SATURDAY, SEPT. 22, 1883.

THIS has been in every way a delightful and interesting day. My opinion, and the opinion of all my fellow-travellers, of the striking grandeur as well as of the unique character of this valley, has been greatly raised.

Early Martin and I rode on excellent ponies to Mirror Lake. The distance was only about three miles, but the part of the valley we traversed very interesting. We followed the line of the Merced River, which is formed high up in the mountains to the east of the valley and is fed by the snow-water. Just now the effects of river and of waterfall are at their worst, owing to the long drought, but I have no difficulty in picturing what a beautiful as well as grand valley this must be in spring when the winter's

MIRROR LAKE, YOSEMITE VALLEY

snow is yielding to the summer's sun and the earth wears its green mantle.

As a lake, Mirror Lake is a failure and a serious failure. When we first saw it this morning, our feeling was one of complete disappointment. Great sandbanks showed us plainly enough that it is of considerable extent when at its best, but to-day it is shrunk into small dimensions and is indeed little better than a stagnant pool.

But lo! the wonders it reflects! It is situated in a bend of the valley where the walls are about one and one-half miles apart. The walls are on one side the North Dome, and on the other Mount Watkin (so called after the photographer) and these rise abruptly from the level, while their polished smooth faces and white appearance readily lend themselves to clear reflection.

We approach the banks of the contracted water, and standing upon a vantage ground of rock we look upon the murky bosom of the lake. It was wonderful. Clearly as possible we see the inverted mountains reflected. Trees, rocks, shrubs ever, deep, deep down in the waters of the Lake. I really felt that I could gaze for hours, occasionally altering my point of view, on this scene, so peculiar and interesting was it. But the most striking incident was yet to happen. Deep down in the heart of the valley sunrise is late; and when it appears in Mirror Lake, it appears close to the top of one of the Lyall Range, which is duly mirrored in the lake. As sunrise approaches, we fix our eyes in the lake at the point where already we see the reflected glow of the coming sun. Presently in the lake deep down we see the glitter as of a great brilliant. Larger and larger it becomes until its brightness dazzles the eye, and you are obliged to look elsewhere—for now the sun has fully risen in the Mirror Lake.

We canter back to breakfast, well satisfied with our morning, and with appetites well calculated to do justice to Mr. Cook's good things.

But even more interesting doings remained to us this day. We are still in the valley. We want to get out of it. We want to get up to the heights and particularly to the height known as Glacier Point. How is this to be done? The glacier rocks rise abruptly behind us, perpendicular as a wall, with here and there pine trees and underwood at intervals clinging to their sides. Yet we are told it is up this rock we are to ride and ride by the *Macaulay* Trail!

The name interested me, and the man, when we finally arrived at his Hotel, situated on the top, at the very point, and learned his history.

He was born some few miles from Randalstown. His name is James Macaulay. He claims no relationship with Mr. P. Macaulay, but I must say he has got exactly the square, rather determined Macaulay face. He worked as a lad at Randalstown Mill and recollects all about the Macaulay family and all about

Rev. Dr. Curoe, Joshua O'Neill, Dr. McDonnell and
the rest. He afterwards went to work in Glasgow,
afterwards on board a Cunard steamer, and finally
came to this country to work as a miner. He under-
took, entirely at his own risk, the making of this track
when he did not possess in all the world $500, and it
ended by costing him about $5,000, equal to £1,000
sterling! He obtained from the State the right to
collect toll for ten years from those using the trail,
but lately the Government have bought up the residue
of his lease and the Macaulay Trail is now open to
all the world. To complete his personal history—he
married a widow, a German a good deal older than
himself, and he has two infant sons, twins, a couple
of years old. He has also a step-son aged about nine
years, and the finest, brightest, and pluckiest little
fellow I have seen for many a day. I wish Bertie
could see the places that youngster rode a big mule
up and down without winking. I am sure Bertie
would be just as plucky if he was brought up amongst
these mountains—scrambling beside precipices since
his cradle, and indeed his very cradle rocked on the
verge of a precipice. Macaulay's Hotel is most picturesquely situated at the top of the trail, and on the
Glacier Point, and it proved to be as cleanly and comfortable as it is picturesque.

The trail (or horse and foot track) is a very remarkable piece of work, not only creditable to the
maker's resolution, but also very remarkable for the

considerable ingenuity it displays. Some idea will already have been gathered of the difficulty of the work from my description of the place; but that difficulty will be perhaps better understood from the fact that to rise 3,000 feet vertically about 4½ miles have to be traversed—equal to 23,760 feet—and still the track is very steep. The ride up on our ponies was not absolutely free from danger; but, so long as the traveller does not lose nerve, the danger is slight. The ponies have the very sensible but slightly disquieting habit of walking to the very edge at the turns in order to make the inclined plane as easy as possible; and as these verges frequently introduce you to an abrupt fall of a very ugly appearance, the ride is not wholly free from excitement. But it was glorious! Every fresh turn, almost, introduced us to fresh views of this wonderful place; and I affirm that, until I rode this trail and found myself looking down and around me from Glacier Point, I had no adequate idea of the beauty and grandeur of the Yosemite district. The views were superb, and indeed comprehended *all* the views to be seen closer in the valley—the Mirror Lake, the Nevada and Verrall Falls, the Cloud's Rest, and so on.

For the benefit of all future visitors to Yosemite I wish to record my experience that they ought to go direct to Macaulay's Hotel, Glacier Point, see the sunset from Sentinel Dome, stay the night there, and thence proceed to the valley—if so inclined—after-

wards. The walk down the trail is not at all labouri-
ous, while the walk up is a very serious undertaking
except for the young and active. At present railway
and hotel interests are combined to send the visitors
direct into the valley and to keep them there as long
as possible. I affirm that this is not the way to see the
Yosemite to the best advantage.

I have said Macaulay's Hotel was picturesquely
situated: it is—startlingly so. My excellent bedroom
on the first floor was approached by a ladder and balcony on the valley side of the house. I declare I am
not exaggerating when I say that upon opening my
door to come out it looked as if, should I miss my
foot, I should be hurled into the valley three thousand feet below.

I afterwards went to the verge of the cliff or point
where very stout iron bars had been placed to remove
any possibility of danger. It was appalling. If I
dropped my stick, it would fall plumb with the rock
to its base. The cattle in the plain below were the
merest specks. Fancy a perpendicular descent about
ten times (I should say) the height of Nelson's
Pillar!

Later on, escorted by young Jules (his mother is a
native of Strasburg), we rode up to the tip-top of Sentinel Dome to see the sunset. The sunset effects, as
a matter of colour, were not grand, but the view all
round the horizon was strikingly beautiful and well
repaid our efforts. The clear grey light of evening

seemed to bring out into clearer outline the varied peaks and crags and fantastic shapes of the mountains all round the horizon, and showed, away to the east and north, the vague forms of mountain upon mountain until they became undistinguishable from the clouds. We were looking upon the great Sierra Nevada Range.

Something attempted and done had earned for us a good night's rest;[1] and we got it. I should desire no better accommodation in every way than James Macaulay and his wife afforded us.

SUNDAY, SEPT. 23, 1883.

THE stage was to start at 9 o'clock to take on Martin and myself and any passengers who should ride up the Macaulay Track from the valley.

We were up and about at 5 o'clock, drinking in this wonderful air and enjoying from the hotel balcony one of the finest views the neighbourhood affords. I told the seven passengers who came panting from below in time to catch the stage what they had missed, joined with them in insisting that the stage should wait until they had, at the least, the opportunity of seeing the view from Glacier Point, and finally made

[1]Something attempted, something done,
Has earned a night's repose.
                    —LONGFELLOW's *Village Blacksmith.*

them ardent converts to my view that the proper way
to enter the valley and to enjoy it is *via* Macaulay's
Hotel and Glacier Point.

The first stage of our journey towards Clark's was
new to us. It covered a distance of about fourteen
miles to a place called Chincopin. It was through a
beautiful natural country, charmingly wooded and
undulating, but as dry as a parched pea.

Arrived at Clark's at 2.30. There still remained
something more to do—namely, to see Mariposa
Grove, where the big trees are to be seen. A trunk of
a tree from this spot is, I think, on view in the Crystal Palace. I had resolved *not* to see this sight unless
I could go on horseback. I was, and I am, heartily
sick of American staging. I succeeded in getting a
very excellent black mare and had a most enjoyable
ride of about eighteen miles there and back. The
trees are awfully big, and there are a great many of
them scattered over the forest; but that said, all is
said. There was nothing particularly interesting
about them. A space through one of them was cut
sufficiently wide for the stage and six horses to drive;
and in many of them there were holes big enough to
shelter me and my horse from rain, had rain
happily fallen. Still these are *not* the *boss* trees of the
world. There are, I believe, some at Teneriffe even
larger.

I want to say a word about the merits of my bonny
black mare. With us, as you know, walking, trotting,

and cantering are the paces most cultivated in our roadsters and hacks. Well, my black was first class at walking and cantering, but as bad a trotter as any one could desire. She had, however, *two* paces utterly unknown amongst our horses, called here "one footing" and "three footing," which, although not elegant to look at, are easy to the rider and help over the ground at from five to six miles the hour.

Altogether I had through the pine forests a charming ride and one comparatively free from dust—that pest of American country life in the advanced summer and early autumn.

MONDAY, SEPT. 24, 1883.

WE started from Clark's and retraced our steps in the stage via Fish Camp, Fresno Flats, and Goldmine Gulch to Mace's Hotel and Madera. There was nothing noticeable *en route*. We had secured the front seats by the driver, and therefore suffered comparatively little from the dust, but greatly from the intense heat—quite 98° in the shade.

I was not sorry when we reached Mace's Hotel, Madera, and had so reached the end of our staging, with which I am not in love. Mr. Mace, by the way, weighs 350 pounds, which means 25 stone English.

TUESDAY, SEPT. 25, 1883.

WE were astir this morning at 4 A.M., as our train left Madera at 5 o'clock, arriving in San Francisco at 12.30 P.M.

Looking back on all the incidents of this Yosemite Expedition, covering some six days, I ask myself has it indeed been a *pleasure* or a *pain?* And the answer is by no means clear.

On the whole, looking back, I am glad I have seen the Yosemite, but, could I have foreseen the physical labour and the disagreeableness involved, I should certainly not have gone. I advise my friends not to go until a railway has reduced the staging distance, which is now about 100 miles, to at most a fifth of that distance. Again I advise them *not* to go in the summer or autumn. I am sure it is an enchanting and marvellous spot when the streams and rivers and falls are full and when, free from dust, vegetation of all kinds, on mountain and in dale, in tree and in flower, is freshest and brightest. I am sure also that to the geologist and the botanist it must afford a world of interest; and several times during this trip I have found myself regretting that I did not know at least a little something of both botany and geology. Learn from this, O ye young! while there is yet time, to cultivate extended tastes. They will be a pleasure to you always, but especially a pleasure and an added interest when, later in life, you come to travel.

So ends the story of our Yosemite Expedition.

I am not sorry to find myself, as I write, within reach of the Bath of the Turk and the street tramcar —free from jolting—of the white man.

WEDNESDAY, SEPT. 26, 1883.

SAN FRANCISCO en route for Salt Lake City. I am writing in difficulties and in face of a great disaster! I have lost my notebook! And now, on Thursday, October 4th, I am sitting down to try to reproduce from memory the incidents of eight days. My usage is to note from day to day anything notable that occurs and then write my despatch when I get to steady quarters at my hotel. Now and then I try the train, but it is too shaky, at least for me. I am writing at the Southern Hotel, St. Louis—having left S. 'Frisco on the date a-top.

Even now at St. Louis we are little more than halfway across this great continent on our way to the Eastern Seas—as they are here called. I went this morning to the Hibernian Bank, where I heard Joshua O'Neill was a principal bookkeeper—I mean Joshua O'Neill, formerly Mr. Macaulay's bookkeeper at the Randalstown Mills. The poor fellow was very glad to see me and seemed greatly gratified at my calling. I think I should have known him, though he is greatly changed and aged. He is now almost alone in the world: he has only one surviving

daughter. He enquired in the kindest way for Mr.
Macaulay, Mrs. Macaulay, and their children. He
was greatly grieved to hear of Mr. Macaulay's death.
I told him how well Charles and Colman had got on
—especially Colman—and he seemed delighted. He
was full of gratitude to Mother Mary Baptist Russell, to whom he says he owes not only his present
position, but the first start he got in San Francisco in
other employment. He does not on the whole think
very much of the *tone* of American life. He says
there is very little faith or religious feeling in the
country except amongst the Catholics, and that very
many of these are careless and lukewarm. So far as
I can gather, there is no place in the United States
in which on the whole the Catholic body, or, in other
words, the Irish Catholic body, stand so well as in
San Francisco in point of religious organization, education, mercantile, social, and political position.

I spent all yesterday afternoon and the greater part
of to-day with Kate. At St. Mary's Hospital the
children of their schools—bright, healthy, intelligent-
looking children they were—went through certain
calisthenic and musical exercises very pleasant to see
and to hear. As to the latter, I was rather surprised
when the pianist who accompanied the singers struck
up the English national anthem of Dr. John Ball. I
was surprised. "God save the Queen" here in a Republican country! However, my surprise soon
ceased, for the accompanying song was an ode to

America entitled "America," and which as a national air ranks close after "The Star Spangled Banner."

I also went through the hospital wards. They are bright, cheery, and wonderfully neat and clean. They have wards for the poor and also for those who can pay for higher class accommodation. Their patients are frequently Protestants—indeed, Kate says she knows the Protestant Bishop very well from the fact of his frequently coming to visit his co-religionists and subjects in the wards.

Later we drove (that is, Kate, Sister Mary Aquin Martin, James Gartlan and myself) in the convent carriage-and-pair (!) to the Penitents' Home and the Reformatory, at Potrero Avenue, on the outskirts of the city. Our driver was a rum old fellow—a Dundalk man, whose name I forget, but who has purchased a home under the care of the Sisters for life! He occasionally, when it suits his dignity, officiates as coachman—I beg his pardon, as driver.

The establishment at Potrero was most interesting, and it is worth noting that as regards the inmates of the Reformatory School these are committed to the care of the good Sisters by the State authorities, who pay for each child or at least contribute to the support of each child.

I think I have already mentioned poor old Miss Kate Russell, one of the three[1] sisters formerly of Elm Hall, Dublin, who lived many years in Cincin-

[1]In reality there were six sisters.

nati. She is the last survivor. She is a ladylike, handsome old person who is ending her days with Kate in cheerfulness and peace.

She was delighted to see me and seemed to feel the leave-taking a good deal. She thought me very like Kate, but my face seemed to awaken old memories, some sweet and some bitter, no doubt, that probably long had slept. Poor, dear old soul! God has anyway given her a quiet evening for her life.

One interesting spot, and a sad one in some sort, too, is the Sisters' Grave Ground at Potrero. Here on the bright hillside under the shadow of the maple tree and the cottonwood rest nearly one-half of that devoted band whom Kate led now nearly 30 years ago from the Old World to the New, carrying the Cross with them.

San Francisco—California indeed—has a very old Catholic history. It was here years ago, when Spain was still a great power and her people an adventurous race, that the great Christian symbol was planted by Juan Cobrillo in 1542—nearly half a century before Drake sailed into San Francisco. It was here, too, that in 1770 was founded the great Franciscan Mission under Father Francis Junipero Serra, which has left its mark even until now. Indeed the name of the great city of the South is that of the Patron Saint of the Missionaries, and was given to it by Father Juan Crespi and Francisco Gomez in 1770 with the assent of Gaspar de Portolá, Governor for Spain of Lower

California. I have read some quaint appreciative lines of Bret Harte on this point.

The traces of the old Spanish occupation amongst the people are few. Many of the Spanish names of places survive, and Mission Bay, in the greater San Franciscan Bay, still marks the spot where the pioneer missionaries spent their lives in the service of the Great Master. One of the old mission churches survives here—adobe-built. This kind of building needs explanation: It consists of bricks which are not fire-dried and which are joined or built together by a mud-cement made of the same clay of which they are made, until the whole becomes a homogeneous consolidated mass. Farther south, namely at Monterey, along the coast, are the ruins of a very fine church built in connection with the San Carlos or Carmel Mission of that place and which dates back to the epoch of the Father Serra before mentioned.

We dined at San Francisco with a Mr. Oliver, a great friend of Mother Mary Baptist, a warm-hearted and genuine Irishman and Catholic. He is one of the many millionaires of this place. We met several representative Irishmen and Catholics. Amongst them Mr. Tobin, Sr., and Mr. (or Colonel) Tobin, Jr., father and son, who are respectable lawyers here. There were many shades of political opinion expressed and represented, from pure Whiggism to ultra-Parnellism or perhaps more properly Healyism. We agreed in two things, however:

the first that at bottom there is little love for England amongst the American people, and secondly that amongst the majority of the Irish of all classes and positions the feeling is one of implacable, irreconcilable hatred of England. It is a mistake, too, to suppose that this feeling is confined to the lower order or to what may be described as the rowdy element. Far from it; it extends to men of means, of education and position, who are utterly opposed to politicians of the dynamite and murder calibre. Colonel Tobin said that he had no doubt that in San Francisco alone he could raise at least 12,000 men who, without thought of pay or of consequences to themselves or their business, would fight in any war by the side of any people against England. I doubt if there be much exaggeration in this statement. It is to be recollected at the same time that what is pointed at is no Irish rising—for on all hands it is admitted that *that* is out of the question. It is the old story—the old cry —"England's difficulty is Ireland's opportunity."

The position of the Irish in San Francisco is very strong. Probably it is stronger in San Francisco and in Chicago than elsewhere in the United States. Their influence is considerable and legitimate. They show generally on this continent the wretched love for Government place that distinguishes them at home—in common be it said with their Scotch brethren. Their great competitors for place here are the Germans, and the race between these nationalities for place is close and exciting. The native Americans are not in it with them.

Of the position of the Irish in the State of New York I shall have to speak very differently by and by.

I left poor Kate very sad, poor soul, but greatly pleased at having had the Old Land brought closer to her by my presence. God bless her and all the Sisterhood, who promised to pray very steadily for me and for mine. By the way, as Kate was the Rev. Mother, I was promptly dubbed "Uncle"—but without the "Reverend."

We left San Francisco at about 4 o'clock P.M., *via* Oakland, and intending to follow the most picturesque route eastward that this continent affords, that is, over the Wassatch, Sierra Nevada, and Rocky ranges of mountains by Reno, Truckee, Ogden, Salt Lake City, Newton, Topeka, Kansas, and Kansas City to St. Louis and thence *via* Philadelphia to New York. I have already described in my earlier Letters the ascent of the Rockies many hundreds of miles farther north along the line of the Northern Pacific Railway; and I will now confine myself to what is or seems to me peculiar to this route.

We found ourselves, when morning broke upon us in our sleepers, not far from a small city rejoicing in the name of Winnemuca and found that our engines —for there were two—were bravely fighting their way up the ascent which marks the great Divide of the Pacific Slopes.

THURSDAY, SEPT. 27, 1883.

FROM morning to night we were speeding through a country with every variety of scenery. In places bleak, sterile, and unlovely, with that glazed look upon the surface which indicates the presence of alkaline matter and marks the unsuitability of the land for agricultural purposes. In other places a great combination of mountain and lake, with a new revelation of wonderfully beautiful colouring in rock and tree and general landscape. I say a *new* revelation, for now the autumn tints for the first time are noticeable by us. The change was marked and sudden. On the Pacific Slopes there was little evidence that winter is rapidly overtaking us; but we had barely passed the summit of Wassatch Mountains till the winter hues were general and unmistakable. Some of the colours were unlike anything with us. For instance, the cottonwood tree and a species of maple, which were common, had their leaves new-coloured a bright yellow, which in combination with all manner of tints from deep crimson to green and against a background of red sandstone and limestone and gypsum was striking and effective. When morning came, we were far in the State of Utah—the kingdom of the Latter Day or Mormon Saints. At Ogden we found ourselves skirting that curious physical phenomenon not yet even fully explained, a great lake of salt water—briny as the Atlantic—

many miles from the sea.   It is so dense that it is said
that no one sinks in it; and to the same cause is attributed the fact—for fact it is—that, while the wind
is sufficient to lash with fury adjoining waters, the
surface of the Salt Lake is calm and unruffled.

Finally we arrived at Salt Lake at 10 A.M.

SALT LAKE CITY, FRIDAY, SEPT. 28, 1883.

THE city is certainly picturesquely situated and
laid out.   The streets are very wide, are generally planted with trees, and have in many cases rivu-
lets running at their sides; and in the case of the principal streets lead towards hills which rise from the
plain at some distance from the city.   The buildings,
too, are frequently imposing and always neat, freshly
painted and attractive.

The population is about 25,000, and of this it is
not claimed by the Gentiles that they number more
than 5,000.   In justice it is to be said that Salt Lake
is a peaceable city, and, generally speaking, free from
crime.   I believe the police amount to less than ten.
All the city officers from the Mayor (Jennings) down
are held without any exception, I believe, by the Mormons; while as to the States (meaning the United
States) offices they are given to the Gentiles.   Between the government of the United States and the
Mormons there is something like war.   Congress de-
clines to accept Utah into the confederation of the

States, principally if not wholly because of the polygamistic practices amongst the Mormons. They know
that, if made a State, the Governorship and all the
higher offices would be held by Mormons. At present it remains a "Territory" merely, which leaves the
governing State appointments in the hands of the
President of the United States. The Congress has,
by what are known as the Edmunds Laws, striven in
earnest to put down polygamy, but hitherto with little effect. The law is evaded and practically set at
naught. One conviction, and one only, has been obtained, and that in the case of a Mr. Reynolds, who
admitted polygamy in order to test the validity, con-
stitutionally, of the Edmunds Law. It is a sore point
with the Mormons that, notwithstanding promises to
the contrary, President Hayes left the convicted man
to work out his full period of sentence. The Mormons further complain that the Edmunds Law is con-
demnable because *ex post facto*—that is, that by its
retrospective action it makes that penal and criminal
which, when done, was not either. In other words,
they say that at best it should be directed against
polygamistic marriages in the future. A Mr. Cannon, who had served in Congress for several years as
Senator—a leading Mormon—was unseated and declared disqualified by a majority of votes in Congress
on the ground of polygamy. I met this Mr. Cannon
later at the house of the present President and
Prophet of the Mormon body, Mr. Taylor. Mr.

Cannon, like Mr. Taylor, is a plain, very commonplace kind of person: I could discern no sign of the
prophet or apostle in either. Mr. Cannon is about
fifty-five years of age and Mr. Taylor is about sev-
enty-three. Mr. Taylor is a venerable-looking, grey-
haired man, very prosaic, free from all affectation,
puts on no prophetic or apostolic airs, and is thoroughly commonplace. I had hoped for the opportunity of some close conversation with these gentlemen, but the advent of a lady visitor forbade this, and
I shortly after took my leave.

The faith of the Mormons negatively and posi-
tively may be summed up thus:

1. They believe in the Bible, generally; but have

2. Special belief in the Revelations to their
prophet and founder, Joseph Smith, and to Brigham
Young and any subsequent prophet. These (so far)
are contained in the Mormon books.

3. Belief in Baptism by immersion, as washing
away sin, but disbelief in original sin.

4. Belief in vicarious Baptism for the dead, and
(I believe) also for the living.

5. Belief in the efficiency of laying on of hands.
Their affairs spiritual are managed by their Prophet
and Apostles—who look after (and that pretty
sharply) the temporal matters pertaining to their
church.

They exact, or more correctly they expect, each
Mormon to pay into the treasury a tithe or tenth of

the earnings. Thus a man earning 75 dollars a month pays monthly 7½ dollars, and so on. It is not a payment in respect of *net* profits merely. Many of the weak-kneed brethren have succumbed under this test of their faith. Thus the proprietors of our hotel were Brothers Walker, who gave up Mormonism only (it is said) because the ten per cent. bore too heavily upon them. There is no doubt that this tithing brings enormous sums into the treasury and gives to its controllers enormous power. Indeed there is a firm belief among Gentiles and ex-Mormons that the prophets and apostles grow fat upon the tithing. Of the truth of this belief I cannot speak.

The tithing-house is one of the features of the place. Here are not only offices for money payments, but granaries, etc., for the reception of tithing in kind and weighing machines for testing its accuracy. The other striking Mormon buildings are the Temple, built of granite, and imposing but not religious in character. It is incomplete. The Tabernacle where the body habitually worship is a curious building, in shape like an inverted boat. It can seat some 4,000 people, and is said to be remarkable for its fine acoustic properties. I met the Chief Justice (Hunter), the great legal functionary of the Territory, and had with him an interesting conversation. He had just been delivering a forcible address to the Grand Jury on the necessity of vindicating the law in the matter of the Edmunds legislation; but in private he did not speak hopefully of what could be done. A shrewd observer afterwards remarked it wouldn't be law which would break up Mormonism. He looked to the spread of intelligence; to the rebellion which he thinks is sure to come against the tithing, and to the influence of Gentile tastes and fashions and the artistic efforts of a few French modistes, to do more to break up the superstition than the law will do. I had a long conversation with two Mormon men, but not, to my regret, with any Mormon women. I should have greatly liked to converse in confidence with the first or second of a series of (say) six or eight wives. It is a mistake, however, to suppose that polygamy is universal or anything like universal amongst them. It is really only the well-to-do who will be allowed to practise it, and not always, it is said, even these. Gentiles tell me that the women appear to be the strongest advocates for this strange condition, and their zeal, if it be real, is explained thus: In the scheme of creation woman was a mere afterthought. Of herself she is nothing, and, unless she is the real wife or is sealed to man, her chances of eternal glory are small. I need not point out that this creed has a markedly masculine character, but these poor women or many of them believe in it. The women amongst the Mormons are said to be heavily worked, and one explanation of polygamy here was thus given: "Wages run very high, and if a man can get a wife to do his cooking comfortably and ask no wage, and another to do his washing on the same terms, and another to milk the cows and make the butter, why, there's great economy in polygamy."

The two men I alluded to above are a Scotchman and an Englishman. The Scotchman is John Aird of Kilmarnock, now nearly seventy years of age. I believe he is thoroughly sincere, but I think he has got a bee in his bonnet. He left his Scotch wife in Scotland (she wouldn't come with him), but he contributes to her support, and he has married what he calls his first true wife in Mormondom, and he told us his Mormon wife is now urging him to marry a third with a view to his greater glory in the Kingdom to come. He affirms that he was instantly cured of sciatica by the laying on of hands of one of the apostles, and that on the occasion when he was baptised by immersion a special miracle was wrought for a sign to him. He asserted that, when he went to the Scotch burn for baptism, the wind was raging and the water, but that when he got into the water a calm followed, whereas upon his emerging the storm began again. I mildly suggested that with his head under water he could not probably notice the state of wind and water; but this prosaic explanation he would not have. His special "fad" or mission is to get baptised for the benefit of his friends. He says he has about 200 in his book for whom, before he dies, he intends to get baptised; and included in the number is his recalcitrant Scotch wife, who, though she takes his money, he says never writes to him to acknowledge it.

The Englishman was W. T. Ayland of Birmingham. I think he was sincere, but again I thought he had a slate off. He was a workingman who had married a second wife—the two wives, as he expressed it, "living together like sisters." He did admit on cross-examination that his first wife objected to his second marriage; but afterwards "she came into it" and they had since got on very well together. "What reconciled your wife to this second marriage?" I asked. "Oh! religion," he promptly answered; "she knew it would be for the greater glory of my second wife and for my own." I do not think the man was aware he was uttering stupid, beastly cant.

I asked Chief Justice Hunter, who struck me as being a remarkably intelligent, clear-headed man, as to the nationalities of which Mormonism is made up. He said principally Scandinavian, Welsh, and English. "Are there any Irish?" I asked. "Yes, a few," he replied; and he referred me to James Dwyer, a bookseller. I went there. He says he was born in this country in Rochester, but he looked and spoke very like an Irishman born in his native country. He was a regular humbug, in my opinion, and I could not avoid the suspicion that in his case, regard for the *profits*, at least as much as for the *prophets*, actuated him; but I may be doing the man an injustice. He is the Mormon bookseller of the place.

We went to a very nice theatre and saw performed by the Union Square Company of New York a very good piece called "Paris Flats."

SATURDAY, SEPT. 29, 1883.

WE left on this morning at 10.30 *en route* through the Rockies for Denver, the capital of Colorado. I have already told you the incidents of the ascent of the Rockies when going from east to west by the Northern Pacific and I will not therefore dwell on this in detail.

The line of railway is probably the most daring ever laid out by an enterprising engineer. Its gradients are in places very steep, and its curves the sharpest by far I ever saw. I am not exaggerating when I say that, standing on the steps of the train platform, which commands a view forward and backward, I have frequently lost the engine round one curve and the tail of the train round another. Add to this the fact that the train runs on the narrow gauge, and you will understand that there were some "jumpy" elements about our journey. But all the same a gloriously picturesque line it is. Marshall's Pass, the summit point the train attains in the Rockies, is 10,700 feet above the level of the sea; and if you will just look at the height of the highest mountain in Ireland, you will have some idea of what these figures mean. The view from it was very fine. The day was clear, and below us lay to the east what seemed an interminable succession of mountains, varied here and there by lake and plain and forest. Early as it is in the autumn, the railway men were busy at work in repairing and building up the snow-sheds, for the snowfall is here at times so enormous as to wholly block the line if unprotected. For miles we passed through wooden tunnels (with spaces here and there) built up with great strength. The snowfall had helped to blight whole miles of young forest trees which had bent and given way under their snowy burthen.

As we were descending from the summit towards the east, a startling incident occurred. A great boulder came tumbling down the hillside, just clear of the engine and tender, and, blocking the wheels of one of the passenger cars, upset it (full of passengers) in an instant. But the engineer had already seen the danger, and, before the succeeding cars could run into the overthrown one, the brakes had acted and we were brought to a standstill almost instantaneously. The men and women and little ones had to be lifted through the window; for, you must understand, the doors of the American railway cars are all at the ends and none of them at the sides. Several men and women were more or less badly hurt and shaken, but no life was lost and no limb broken. Two young ladies of the theatrical party (who were journeying home to New York) exerted themselves ad-

mirably in looking after the invalids: no Sisters of
Mercy could have done better.

In about two hours' time we were again careering
downhill and uphill and round sharp curves, just as if
nothing had happened. The most striking sight on
our journey we had yet to see—by far the most striking—namely the Grand Cañon.

It was twilight when we first entered it; and if this
prevented our seeing it with the same close accuracy,
it undoubtedly left more to the imagination. It was
startling. For several miles the train, following the
line of the Arkansas River, winds in and out and
round and about a long series of jutting, perpendicular rocks such as I have never before seen to anything like the same extent. There were no slopes with
vegetation; no patches of green; all was rock and
nothing but rock rising wall-like on each side of the
river, side by side with which and only a few feet
above which our train ran. The effect was indeed
startling. Looking up as it were from this cleft in
the rocks, we saw the stars above our heads—looking
back, we did not see the opening through which we had
come, for we had just sharply rounded a curve—looking forward, there was no opening for us out apparent.
We seemed completely hemmed in, and yet we were
rattling along at the rate of about 25 miles an hour.
The physical conformation of the place is remarkable. It looked literally as if the water had through
the course of ages worn out this way for itself in the

rocks, deepening it more and more the more it ran. I do not know the height of the rocks, but in places certainly several hundred feet in height; while the Cañon or Gorge was not in width apparently more than fifty to seventy feet.

SUNDAY, SEPT. 30, 1883.

So we went on, on, through the Sunday—no church for us to-day—past Montrose, Gunnison, and Pueblo, past Colorado Springs and on towards Denver.

From Pueblo towards Denver was out of our route to the east. I made the detour in order to try and see William Dillon, formerly at the Irish Bar and brother of John Dillon. You will recollect his dining with us in Harley St. He is in partnership with a man named Ratcliffe in a cattle ranch at Sedalia or rather near Sedalia, a little town twenty-five miles south and short of Denver. I thought George Fottrell and Mrs. Fottrell would like to hear about him, and I was anxious to see him on my own account. Martin and Darling stopped at Colorado Springs, but I went on to Sedalia. The train ought to have been at Sedalia at 7 o'clock; it was not there, in fact, till 1 o'clock on Monday morning—1 A.M. I mean. Cold and perished I arrived at Sedalia and found not only William Dillon and his partner, Mr. Ratcliffe, awaiting me, but also Mr. Thomas Fottrell, formerly in the Hibernian Bank, Monaghan—the brother of Mrs. Power.

MONDAY, OCTOBER 1, 1883.

ONE A.M. to-day, as I have already said, found me at Sedalia; a few minutes sufficed to find us all, *i.e.*, Dillon, Ratcliffe, and myself (for Fottrell was starting next morning by early train) in Mr. Ratcliffe's two-horse buggy, and rattling away under the light of the stars to our destination nine miles off— Spring's Ranch.

Here a cheery sight awaited us. Mrs. Ratcliffe had a bright log-fire burning and an appetising supper ready, after discussing which I promptly tumbled into bed, for I had only one day here (this very Monday) and I wanted to make the most of it.

Once for all let me say I was the guest of Mrs. Ratcliffe, and if her treatment of me was anything like what one may ordinarily expect in ranch life—then ranch life is *not* difficult to put up with.

Dillon looked remarkably well and stronger, broader-shouldered and in every way bigger than I expected to find him. He came out three years ago for his health, and had the good luck to be taken as boarder by Mr. Ratcliffe. Last June twelve-month (that is, June, 1882) he may fairly be said to have entered upon ranch life on his own account. Mr. R.

has his own ranch, but they (D. and he) have taken a ranch which they work in partnership. So far the experiment seems to have answered wonderfully well, not only as to health, but also as to profits—considering that their ranching is not on a very large scale. Dillon has his own house and establishment on the partnership ranch, quite good enough for bachelor quarters, but not quite up to the mark of Mrs. Ratcliffe's comfortable, not to say, luxurious quarters. Dillon's household retinue consists of one woman (from Sligo, I think) named Doyle, who is cook and housekeeper and maid of all work. Doyle is a trusty soul, and I believe devoted to her master, but his principal amusement consists in abusing the ways and manners of the New and asserting the marked superiority of the ways and manners of the "Ould Counthry." I must here break off or I'll have no fair chance of being read. I will give a sketch of this beautiful, bracing place in my next.

SEDALIA, MONDAY, OCT. 1, 1883 (*continued*).

ALTHOUGH it was quite 3 o'clock when we got to bed, we were up again before 8 o'clock and in the saddle before 9.30 o'clock. I was bound to rejoin Martin on Tuesday, and was therefore resolved upon making the most of my day.

By the way, the saddles in the northern and also in the western parts of this continent (I cannot yet speak

of the east) are very different from ours, and the seat
of the rider very different also. The saddles here
offer much greater support to the rider, and in this respect they more closely resemble the cavalry and
police saddles at home; but they are much more elaborate than these. In front, instead of our pommel,
is a perpendicular arm not without its advantages as
a support but principally useful as a means of attach-
ing conveniently the lasso or any less interesting rope,
any small baggage, etc., while behind, the saddle rises
abruptly, fixing the seat, so to speak, securely. In
fact, the saddle is such as to compel what we know in
England as the straight or military seat. I have now
ridden a good deal in the north and west in this saddle, and like it greatly. The girthing arrangements
are much more elaborate than with us, and the stirrup
leathers at first sight seem unnecessarily cumbersome
until it is explained that they are devised to protect
the feet and in great measure the legs riding through
long grass and in brushwood.

Nothing could exceed the delicious character of
the morning. The sun was bright, the air clear, crisp,
and bracing, and the sky was wholly blue—that blue
which I understand to be meant by an Italian sky.
It was perfectly charming in its exhilarating effects
—the very perfection of a climate. D—— assured
me this was the normal condition of things—some
very sharp weather in winter and even in summer, but
never lasting very long and always recurrence to that

which to-day we experienced. The country itself is fairly attractive. The Ratcliffe-Dillon ranch is situated along a range of foothills (foothills to the Rockies) and it is higher above the sea than the highest Irish mountain, namely, it is over 6,000 feet. It is especially well-watered, it is fairly wooded, and the character of the grass is exceptionally good. I am quite learned in the grasses here. They are chiefly three kinds: the wire grass, the gramma or grammar grass (orthography doubtful), and the blue grass or blue stem grass. The last is by far the finest and most nutritious, and in this the Spring's ranch largely abounds. Unlike the grasses with us, which, unless cut and dried, cannot be saved in stacks, but left standing would in our moist climate decompose, the Colorado grass saves itself on its stem—that is, it dries as it stands and so is saved by the climate for the winter's use of the cattle, or it may be cut and stacked on the same day! This, I need hardly say, is owing to the dryness of the atmosphere. This dryness of the atmosphere is the difficulty, the only difficulty, in Colorado. They have little rain and can do little or nothing in the way of cultivation unless they can get water for irrigation. The result is that a soil capable, with irrigation, of producing anything is in great part useless and unproductive. The further result is that every little creek or brook, nay, even every little natural spring that bubbles up from the ground, is eagerly sought, and the land in which it is situated

pre-empted or somehow or other got hold of. In
these cases its use is not with reference to cultivation,
but to provide the needed watering-place for cattle.

The breed of cattle seems good; and good speci-
mens of the English Durham and Hereford breeds
have been introduced with a view of still further improving it. For a wide district comprising Sedalia,
Castle Rock, etc., Denver is the cattle market. Denver is the capital of the State and has risen to be a city
of 90,000 inhabitants, risen indeed all too rapidly,
for a reaction has followed the Denver "boom" and
land is not now nearly so valuable as it was two or
three years ago. So far as I can see, America must
have her booms. A boom will fetch a tradesman from
San Francisco to Portland in Oregon on the chance
of getting four dollars a day wage instead of three
dollars at home. It will bring the trader from east to
extreme west in the hope of finding himself taking
part in the building up of a new and great city. The
other day at Garrison on the Rio Grande, I saw a
broad-shouldered chap at the depôt with his hands in
his pockets and the unmistakable look of the idling
loafer about him.

"What are you doing here?"

"Waiting for the boom."

"What boom?"

"The Garrison boom, I guess."

"What will that do for you?"

"I'm a bricklayer, and the boom means $5 a day."

"What can you get now?"

"Maybe $3½, anyway $3, but I am not going to work for that as long as I've a dollar in my pocket."

"Where did you come from?"

"I came from the State of Maine at the first, but I've been after half a dozen booms since then. I came last from San Francisco."

"Why did you leave San Francisco? Is work short there?"

"Not a bit of it, but I tell you I come after the boom. Besides, there are too many Chinamen there. I think I'll go to Canada. They tell me there's few of them there."

"Have booms paid you?"

"Well, not much. I have not always been in time, and, like this place, I am too soon it seems."

This conversation is almost literally given, and I give it because it is one out of many proofs which have come under my eyes of the complete unfixedness of the working population. They seem to have no attachment to localities except so far as localities offer them wage inducements. No doubt this spirit more than anything will tend over this great wide Continent to level or approximate to levelling the wage market. But this restlessness or unfixedness is not, as I have said, confined to the working class in the ordinary acceptation of that term. It extends so far as I can judge to all classes—tradesmen, miners, merchants, engineers, farmers, lawyers. The farmers, one would think, are particularly fixed to localities. Far from it. In Canada, in the Northwest States, in the southwest States, I have again and again come across persons who, having tried farming or stock-raising in one or two localities and thought they could better themselves elsewhere, have without compunction packed up or "boxed up " their household gods and turned their backs upon the fields and brooks and hills upon which their young eyes had probably first rested. No one can truly say the Americans are sentimental. I could mention places where there is perhaps a superfluity of sentimentalism.

The young men, also, in the eastern States of New England have thoroughly taken to heart the advice of old Horace Greeley. "Go West, young man, go West." To such an extent have they migrated westward that I am assured the female population in the New England States is considerably in excess of the male population.

It is clear that this pushing, energetic, adventurous restlessness, whatever else may be said for it, is calculated greatly to help and has greatly helped the spread of population and settlement throughout the land. I see I've diverged a good deal from the Spring's Cattle Ranch.

It is in extent about 1,400 acres, but each enclosed ranch is supplemented by the right—open equally to all—to graze upon the unsettled Government lands. These are popularly known as "Uncle Sam's" lands.

This right is, of course, of very high importance, but one which year by year has a more limited area to operate upon, as the Government lands are sold. However, as the land with water on it (as I have before explained) is to a great extent bought up, the inducements to settle on the remainder are yearly diminishing, *unless* indeed it is found that the artesian well system can generally be applied with success throughout the States. This is the great question which is agitating Colorado just now. At Denver the artesian wells are supplying the towns, and scientists in this matter affirm that no difficulty exists in bringing them to operation in the rural districts. If so, the question of water for cattle-drinking is solved; but that wider question of water to meet the needs of the thirsty earth for purposes of agriculture will be still unsettled.

We rode through and round the ranch, and through and round several other ranches, including one held by Peter Brennan, an Armagh man, and one of the earliest settlers in the place. We lunched by the side of a running brook, from which we slaked our thirst and promptly disposed of Mrs. R.'s excellent sandwiches.

The close of evening found us near Mr. R.'s house, and after an exceedingly agreeable ride I rather reluctantly gave up the bridle of my little mare, "Peggy," who carried me merrily and well during the day. A game of poker, at which I was badly worsted by the old settler, finished my day's doings, and by

9.30 I was enjoying profoundly the healthy sleep of
a healthily-tired man.

TUESDAY, OCT. 2, 1883.

NEAR the ranch, at the south end of it, is a place
sometimes called Parry's Park (from the early
owner's name) and sometimes Pleasant Park. It is
one of the most picturesque spots I have seen. It is
nearly surrounded with the well-wooded foothills,
from which several cañons open into it, with creeks or
brooks which serve useful as well as beautifying purposes. But the great attraction of the place does not
lie in these. As you approach the spot, you see at
some distance what clearly appear to be the ruined
walls of an ancient and even an important town. The
illusion is perfect. There the remains of an old castle, here what look like the trees of a terrace of
houses. What is it, then? Simply that nature in
some very fantastic mood had thrown the sandstone
rocks into all manner of odd shapes and (if one may
say so) attitudes. As we approached nearer and could
single out the rocks, even I, unimaginative person
that I am, could discover likenesses to all manner of
beasts and to some human beings also. I will not
specify the latter, but there were some remarkable
politicians amongst them. Taken as a whole, the
place was most attractive, and it only needs an enterprising doctor to discover merits in the water, and a
friendly editor to publish them, and its real true

claims as a health resort could not fail to attract the teeming population of Denver in its holidays. I confess, however, if I were ranching here, I should rather have the place as it is.

We were again up betimes this (Tuesday) morning, for I had to catch the early train south to Colorado Springs at Castle Rock, and the drive to Castle Rock is nine miles.

On the way I had several chapters of Mr. R.'s very interesting experiences.

His own story (which he did not tell) is romantic and is mixed up with his early settlement in the north-west.

He is a Derbyshire man, and against the wishes of some at least of her relations he wooed his present wife, and finally, after the manner of Lord Eldon, John Mitchel, and various other distinguished persons at various times, he eloped with her.

Soon after he was obliged to come to America with a view to obtaining a home and settlement for his wife. Her friends took advantage of his absence, kept his letters from her, and for several years he was ignorant whether she lived or was dead. He continued writing, and, probably home vigilance having lulled, one of his letters after several years reached his wife, and she answered it as a wife should. Straightway he returned to England, reclaimed her, and brought her to Colorado. They have a fine family of three daughters and one son, all born on American soil. The eldest daughter reached seventeen years yesterday. They all work, from the mother to the youngest of them, and are bright and active.

Mr. R.'s experiences of this country, and especially of Colorado State, would make a large and interesting novel. He has driven teams between St. Louis and Denver, and he has driven cattle thousands of miles south and west at a time when the Indians were a living terror to the white man, and when you went about very much with your life in your hand. He recollects when the buffalo herd fed on the Ratcliffe-Dillon ranch, when wolves, including the angry grey wolf, were frequently to be seen, and the bear was not an infrequent visitor. Later, too, in more settled times, he recollects when the settlers used to march together to perform any important acts of husbandry, such as reaping, threshing, and even cow-milking, for purposes of mutual defence against the Indian.

The change is certainly very wonderful in a period of about thirty years, or even less.

"Does any one ever die here?" I asked, taking a long draught of the fresh morning air.

"Very few," answered Mr. R. "They had to shoot a man a little further west to give their cemetery a start; and here," he said, pointing to Castle Rock, "they had to hang a man to begin business. That's true."

Later on he pointed out to me, in the neglected corner of the graveyard, the spot where they had buried a thieving Mexican whom they had caught red-handed killing a sheep, and whom they promptly strung up to the first convenient bough.

Meanwhile we had mounted the hill which divides Sedalia and Castle Rock. The Sedalia foothills were sinking at our feet, and behind them was rising the nobler range, snow-topped, of the higher Rockies, while, away to the south, Pike's Peak was just lifting his venerable head within reach of the morning sun. Pike's Peak, be it known, is considerably higher than Mount Baker (see *ante*) and somewhat higher than Tacoma or Rainier, but it does not look as high or as grand as either of these. The principal reasons are: first, that we are looking at this mountain already at an elevation of over 6,000 feet, and second, that it is surrounded on all sides by a chain of hills, of which it is only one and the greatest.

Castle Rock is the chief town of Douglas County; and it is here that the Land Registry is kept. Its custodian is a Mr. Jones, from the south of Ireland, who fills the office of Clerk of the County. On our way to Castle Rock I had a good view of an extensive range of "Uncle Sam's Land," and on which the cattle of many men were feeding, each man's cattle marked with his particular and registered brand. They are "rounded up" or gathered in when wanted for market or for shelter in winter or for fattening purposes at the homesteads.

After bidding my kind friends good-bye I was soon

rattling away south (over the same ground I had travelled on Sunday night) to Colorado Springs.

On the way I met Mr. Henry Lucy of the *Daily News,* travelling with his wife and intending to stay the night at the Springs. They are on their way for a five months' tour to Japan and home by India and Eastern Europe.

Colorado Springs is a very pretty place, beautifully laid out and planted with trees in all directions and with quite a number of handsome buildings; but the springs are a delusion. These are at Manitou, some four miles off, close at the foot of Pike's Peak. We drove down there later in the day. The sulphur and soda springs, the latter coming up freshly aerated from the earth, are very curious.

On the top of Pike's Peak is a Government observatory in which a scientist is always stationed, night and day, summer and winter, for the purposes of observation. It is indeed from the observations here made, and similar data gathered in a like way, that the American weather predictions, now so famous, are compiled. The service is so severe that no man remains longer on the Peak than a year; and that is long enough, too, when it is remembered that for many weeks at a time it is often impossible to maintain any carrying or directly human communication with the world below. I note here a curious fact touching the highly rarefied condition of the air a-top. A fierce wind will be blowing there which, if met below, would blow you from your legs, and yet (owing to its less density on the high mountain peak) is comparatively little felt.

Later in the evening I rejoined Martin and Darling, and with them went still away south as far as Pueblo, whence we resume our easterly route *via* Kansas and Ohio States, east.

WEDNESDAY, OCT. 3, 1883.

A ROUGHISH road and a bad place in the Pullman sleeper gave us but an indifferent night's rest, and we were not sorry when an early call for breakfast at Newtown in Kansas claimed attention, though the meal itself was poor enough. On we go on our way to St. Louis (our first resting-place), dining at Topeka (still in Kansas) and finally reaching Kansas City, which is situated on the Kansas River, the dividing line between Kansas and Missouri States.

There is a marked difference between these adjoining States, Colorado and Kansas. The former is principally a stock-raising State, the latter is every day becoming more and more a cultivated agricultural State. Kansas seems remarkably rich in its soil, and a great rush of migration has lately set towards it. It has no doubt a great future.

We dined at Topeka, and night found us in our sleeper, speeding away through the great State of Missouri, wherein we reached St. Louis at about 7.30 A.M.

St. Louis, Thursday, Oct. 4, 1883.

WE have looked forward with great expectation to our visit here, for besides the ordinary attractions of the great city—the sixth in importance in the United States—the State annual fair was in progress.

Alas for the vanity of all human desires! We were long since warned that all was not as it should be for the sightseer in the matter of weather. Ever since we left the State of Colorado there has been a marked change and for the worse. There all was bright, dry, cheery, and genial, though bracing and even chilly. But through Kansas and Missouri we've been reminded forcibly of that half damp, half foggy, wholly cheerless weather, with which we are pretty well acquainted in England and in Ireland. Here at St. Louis nothing could be worse. The rain was rapidly falling, the air muggy and well charged with "smuts," and the draggled finery of the shops and public buildings and of the people presented a very melancholy and disheartening spectacle. We resolved to go to-night to Pittsburgh, Pennsylvania, on our way to Washington *via* Harrisburgh.

Meanwhile I found that my good friend, Mr. Frank Thomson of Philadelphia, vice-president of the Pennsylvania Railroad Company, had asked Col. Hill, the resident general superintendent of the company at St. Louis, to look after us.

Under his escortage and in his carriage we were
enabled to see a great deal in a short time. St. Louis'
chief wonder is the great bridge across the Mississippi, to which I here again raise my hat—built by
Mr. Eads, who is the engineer of the Panama or
Darien Canal. It is an enormous structure, so built
that on one floor or level the public carriages and traffic pass, and on another level above the railways having depots in the town pass. On one side of the river
is the State of Illinois, while on the other—the city
side—is the State of Missouri. Some idea of the
magnitude and difficulty of the work will be gathered
when it is recollected that the width of the river at
this point is more than half a mile; and that to get secure rock on which to build the piers the architect was
obliged to sink as much as ninety feet below the mud
bed of the river. To my mind the great feature of
the place is the river, which has only just permanently
received the name of the Mississippi, which it re-
tains until it loses itself in the Gulf of Mexico at New
Orleans. A few miles north of St. Louis the great
rivers, the Missouri and the Mississippi, join forces,
and thenceforth the Missouri is no longer known; it
is merged in the Mississippi. Farther on, in the State
of Ohio, these mighty waters gain a further contin-
gent in the Ohio River, which in its turn was made
up of the rivers Alleghany and Monongahela, which
are confluent at Pittsburgh.

St. Louis is a very fine city, and full of fine buildings—the Courthouse, the Washington University, the St. Louis University (Jesuit), and several of the churches being amongst the finest. The mention of the Jesuit college suggests to me to say that there is no city in the United States in which there is a finer or more efficient set of religious and charitable institutions in connection with Catholicism than in St. Louis.

As its name implies, St. Louis was founded by French settlers, as a trading station in 1762, some of whom came up river from New Orleans and some, it is said, down river from Canada. France had then important territory south. The French can now hardly be said to form an independent element in the population, but there is a part of the city which still bears the name of French Town. From St. Louis you can go south to New Orleans by river-boat; and if only time permitted (it takes four days) I should be delighted to make the trip. It is, I am told, most agreeable, especially at this season if you can secure dry weather.

In company with Colonel Hill we visited the Fair, which consists of an exhibition of the products of all kinds, in crops, in manufactures, and in inventions, of the State. There are besides prizes for the best horses, mules, geese, fowls, etc.

The focus point of the people (whom I was most anxious to see) was the amphitheatre—a lightly constructed building capable of seating 40,000, and which to-day, notwithstanding the bad weather, con-

tained not fewer than 30,000. As I have before remarked of other American crowds, so I remark of
this. All were orderly, though noisy, and they were
cheery and good-tempered. I saw nothing approaching a row in any part, and police were not obtrusively
visible. I feel sure we could not gather such a crowd
in Ireland with like results. Again no sign of in-
sobriety in the crowd, though there is always lots of
custom certainly for the drinking saloons. But what
most astonishes me the more I see of the country is
the absence of all signs of poverty on the surface. I
say on the surface, because I know that there are, and
it is inevitable that there should be, some destitutes
in such an enormous community; but everywhere one
sees crowds, and always well clad and apparently well
fed. I have only once been solicited in the United
States by a beggar, and he was a man with a maimed
hand.

The preparations for the Trades' procession, and
especially for the illumination of the city, were of a
most elaborate description; but owing to the wretched
weather both procession and illumination were post-
poned.

We started for Pittsburgh at 7 o'clock P.M., and
through the night were travelling at a good pace
through the States of Illinois and Indiana, past the
towns of Vandalia, Indianapolis, and Effingham, until
finally at 7.40 A.M. we stopped for breakfast at Rich-
mond in Indiana State.

FRIDAY, OCT. 5, 1883.
(*En route* for Pittsburgh)

ON we go again after breakfast through Indiana
State and through the State of Ohio, past the
cities of Piqua, Urbana, Columbus (where we dined
at 1 P.M.), Newark, and finally we reached Pittsburgh at about 7.30 P.M.

Unhappily the rainy weather continued. The atmosphere was heavy and foggy; and altogether it
would be difficult to imagine a greater change in
climate and temperature than we have witnessed in
the last two days. Nor is the change confined to the
climate. Not only is the country looking more and
more cultivated, and more and more peopled, but on
all sides are signs of manufacturing industry of various kinds working at a high pressure. The country is
rich in coal and in iron ore, and along our line we
see the fierce fires of the blast smelting furnaces, of
the rolling mills, and of the brick factories.

Pittsburgh itself is a great manufacturing city, and,
like many of our English towns of the like order,
great natural beauty has been defaced by the hand of
material civilisation. It is situated on two picturesque
rivers, the Monongahela and the Alleghany, which
here, as I have earlier said, coalesce and form the
Ohio River. Beyond the Monongahela the ground
rises abruptly to the height of several hundred feet,
the streets rising in terrace above terrace and being

approached from the lower levels not only by sloping inclines but by elevators on the principle (hydraulic, I think) of those at Scarborough.

As we walked over the bridge from the Alleghany to the Monongahela side last night, the scene was very striking. The river is here very wide, but not deep; and in the darkness of the night the fires which were close to the river's edge seemed to flare up from the river itself and to be continued high up in the air —really along the dark hillside. We met railway trains of the Pennsylvania Railroad Company careering through the streets in all directions in a way quite startling, to one used to the careful ways, in this regard, of the old country. On they went across and along thoroughfares, and crowded thoroughfares, too, and yet (strange to say) accidents are, I learn, not at all common.

At Pittsburgh a pleasant surprise awaited us. Mr. Frank Thomson had sent on his private car from Philadelphia in charge of his man, Joe Green, who stood grinning a kindly welcome to us on our arrival.

Nothing could exceed the comfort of this car; we have nothing in England to which I could refer you for a parallel. Sitting-room and library commanding a fine and unbroken view of the country, large dining-room, comfortable bedrooms and excellent kitchen cooking arrangements over which (as I afterwards found) Joe Green presides with excellent results. Our car was backing into a siding where we were to-morrow morning (Saturday) to be hooked to the end of the 8 o'clock train and comfortably taken to Washington, and on to Harrisburg and Baltimore.

But before morning comes the night, and such a night! As we started early, Joe thought we had better sleep in our luxurious car, and so we went to bed, but not to sleep! Anything more awful than the hidcous babel of sound which reached my ears in the siding you cannot imagine. Bang-bang-clang-clang-shriek-shriek—all the night through. But for the fact that we had had two bad nights' rest, and at the same time two very hard days' work I do not think I could have closed my eyes in unconsciousness, not for a moment. As it was, I did get a little sleep, but so hideously broken in upon that it brought little rest. Never again, even in the most luxurious of cars, shall I pass another night in the siding at the railway depot of a bustling American town—no, not if I know it.

I break off here. I must reserve for my next despatch the incidents of, in many respects, the most interesting journey I have yet had, viz.: from Pittsburgh through the Alleghany Mountains and along the Taranita Valley via Altoona, Tyrone, Harrisburg, and Baltimore to Washington.

SATURDAY, OCT. 6, 1883.
(*En route* Pittsburgh to Washington)

I WAS glad when the morning broke bright and
promising.   A night of grave discomfort was
passed, and a day full of hopeful anticipation begun.
Our car was luxurious, the weather promised well,
and we knew that the journey across the Alleghanies
and along and over noble river after noble river in
quick succession was considered generally as covering
about the finest scenery on the eastern part of this
continent.   Well, the scenery deserved to the full its
high character, but unhappily it was very soon apparent that our weather-luck was about to desert us.   The
clouds gathered rapidly and hung sulkily along the
hill slopes; and before we had traversed many
miles it was but too plain we were in for a bad
day, and the rain was falling rapidly.   It was a
great pity.   Even the murky atmosphere could not
hide from us the singular beauty of the country;
but the beauty was of that kind which to be seen
at its best required warmth and light and plenty of
these.

Generally it may be said that the scenery was of
the rich, cultivated, comfortable kind—although here
and there (as in the ascent and descent of the Alleghany chain) it was striking.   We are in the great
State of Pennsylvania—by far the most important
State in point of manufacturing industries, such as

coal and other ores, and also the seat of great and successful agriculture.

In very many respects I was from time to time reminded of bits of English landscape; but here there was that wonderful brilliancy of autumn leaf-tints which England can make no pretence at equalling. In point of population, also, it seemed comparable with the counties through which say the London and Northwestern Railway with·us runs. Again this suggests a further point of resemblance. The Pennsylvania Railroad is incomparably the best built and maintained and equipped railroad in the United States. Everywhere are the signs of careful, punctilious management, and I very much doubt whether any of the great railways of the Old World are in any respect better built or ballasted or managed than the Pennsylvania system here.

On all sides were apparent the presence of great industries—the freight-trains laden with grain, and coal and iron ore and manufactured products in iron. And from time to time, as we rolled along at express speed, we sighted now the coal-pit, now the smelting furnace, now the rolling mills, now the brick kilns, and so forth. They say that further south (say in Alabama) they can produce iron at considerably cheaper rates than in Pennsylvania, and it may be so. So far as I can see, Pennsylvania has a secure future, even if part of its industry were removed elsewhere; and even this is a remote danger, for a trade once "lo-

cated" is slow to move, and if to-morrow free-trade
were to become the popular cry at the hustings,
Pennsylvanian capital and energy would find a fresh
and no doubt profitable outlet before the absence of
protection could be seriously felt. As regards for-
midable competition from the south, I believe that is
coming, but the conditions of labour and the conditions relatively of capital and labour are there so un-
satisfactory as to make this, too, no more than a very
remote danger.

Starting about 8.30 A.M. we found ourselves at
noon beside the Conemaugh River—a tributary, too,
of the Ohio—and beginning the ascent of the Alleghany Mountains, the last we surmount on our journey eastward. I am not going to prose you with an
account in detail of this ascent. It possessed no features of grandeur at all comparable with the passage
of the Rockies in the State of Montana north, or in
the State of Colorado south; but it had an interest peculiarly its own. The slopes have a refined, cultivated, civilised, tame look about them which, although not of the highest order of scenery, is all the
same pleasant to the eye and agreeably suggestive.
Besides all this the glorious tints of autumn had invested the woods on the hillside with a gorgeousness
quite novel to me. Still the next day was not favourable to seeing this at its best, although I confess to being charmed with it in spite of the descending rain
which subdued its brilliancy. The Horseshoe ascent

is famous in American railway photography and indeed deserves to be. For a distance of about twelve miles we are making an ascent averaging about 106 feet to the mile until we reach Gallitzin (I think), where a lengthy tunnel reminds one of Rugby tunnel or that between Manchester and Doncaster on (I believe) the Midland Route. I mention this tunnel to note the fact that here very much less tunnelling is done than with us. They prefer—at least in the earlier history of the railways—to make even a considerable detour. Later on when the railway has become a success and can afford luxuries and desires to economise time, tunnelling is more frequently resorted to and in the same way gradients lessened and curves made less abrupt.

At Altoona we are fairly on the east side of the Alleghany divide, and in Altoona we recognise a counterpart of Crewe—for Altoona is to the Pennsylvanian Railroad what Crewe is to the London & N. W. Railway—its mighty workshop.

On, on we roll past Tipton, Tyrone, Birmingham, Petersburgh, Lewistown, to Duncannon, where we enter upon another of the many lovely valleys of the country, the Inniato valley, and for about 100 miles our train is running close by the beautiful but not mighty stream which gives its name to the valley.

Still on, on we go until as we approach close to Harrisburg (the capital of the State of Pennsylvania) we cross one of the loveliest, finest, and most

picturesque of the many great rivers—the Susquehanna. I was perfectly charmed with this river—its
width, its great volume of water, its sloping banks, its
luxuriant vegetation, and the wealth and beauty of
colour in its trees. I was indeed delighted with it.
Where we crossed, the river is little short of a mile in
width. Considering the vast extent of this continent
and its great and frequent mountain ranges—many
of them in perpetual winter garb—I ought not perhaps to be surprised; but I am nevertheless constantly surprised at the frequency of wide-spreading,
deep, and rapid rivers. I check my surprise, but as
each new, great river appears to delight me, up comes
my feeling of surprise once more.

I have said Harrisburg is the capital of the State.
It will have been noticed how seldom it is that the
capital of the State is the chief town of the State. For
instance, Albany is the capital of the State of New
York, which has within it the greatest city in the
States; and here again Harrisburg is the capital of
Pennsylvania, which has Philadelphia, the second city
of the States within it. The reasons for this arrange-
ment are partly geographical and partly political.
The geographical reasons have reference to convenience as to central position and so on, but the political
reasons are also strong. It is considered desirable
that the legislative body of each State should not
meet where a particular party is exceptionally strong
in political and general importance. This is a matter

of statesmanship, but, further, the great bulk of the voting power in the State will generally (impelled partly by meaner motives) combine against "locating" the Legislature in the biggest and therefore the most powerful place.

From Harrisburg to Washington *via* Baltimore we saw little, for the night had fallen and it was late when we entered the stately, dignified capital of the United States—named after America's patron saint (if America could own such a weakness) George Washington.

WASHINGTON, SUNDAY, OCT. 7, 1883.

WE were up soon after the sun, and our impressions overnight of the dignity of this great capital city were fortified. It is by far the most elegant city I have seen in the States, with an air, too, of refinement about it which is not to be found in all cities. For instance, with all its great commercial importance, Chicago is "sweaty" and smells somehow of pig; San Francisco with all its brightness and potentialities in the future has still the *nouveau riche* flavour; and New York, centre at once of commercial and intellectual activity, has an air of restless unrest about it—a feeling of feverishness, as if the spirit of Wall Street had leavened all its society.

St. Matthew's Church, which we visited early in the morning, presented some novel features in a house for Catholic worship. The hateful pew system covered the whole place. But worse—with hardly an exception, the pews were locked! After some searching I got into one, but soon after a lady entered, probably its proprietor, who looked at me as if very little would induce her to bring an action for trespass against me *quare clausum fregit*. It was a novel, wholly novel, experience. I enquired of a lady as we left the church, "Are there any free seats?"

"No."

"Are there any people in Washington who are too poor to pay for a pew?"

"Oh, yes, no doubt."

"What becomes of them?"

"I don't know, they go elsewhere. This is not the only church. This is the fashionable church. It is here the representatives of the various Catholic Legations come to Mass. If one did not lock the pews, you would have no use of the pew you pay for."

I spent the day perambulating the city and sailing on the steamboats that ferry passengers up and down and across the Potomac, on whose eastern bank the city stands. The day was most enjoyable, and the crisp, bright atmosphere helped to bring out the beauty of the public buildings sharply and clearly.

The public buildings are very fine: the Treasury, the Post Office Department, the Army and Navy—all planned in a sensible, practical spirit, but possessing besides considerable architectural beauty. The white marble, granite, and red sandstone, of which the town is built, present an agreeable variety; and the trees which are growing in all parts, and the open public planted spaces, which are numerous, combine to give an appearance of quiet elegance which I have rarely met with, even in the old cities of the Old World. I expect in fifty years Washington will compare favourably with any city in the world. At present it looks as if it had not been built up as speedily as its founders expected, but I learn that wealthy men from other parts of the States are beginning—apart from politics—to take up their residences there, and that the refinement of its society is beginning to be recognised. Just now, too, there is a big scheme on foot to reclaim permanently from the river large, shallow, covered mudbanks, which will at once add considerably to the space available for public purposes and also to the healthful character of the city.

Opposite to Washington, on the other side of the Potomac, is the residence of the late General Lee, who fought so gallantly and brilliantly for the South. It is a hopeful sign to note that all without distinction of North or South refer with pride to the bravery and skill manifested in the War of Secession. Some miles down the Potomac, on its way to Chesapeake Bav, is Mount Vernon, once Washington's residence, but now national property, where are gathered together some precious relics of the great soldier-statesman of America; but I was not able to go down to see it.

Here in the city is to be seen, lifting up its head higher and higher towards the sky, a very noble monument to his memory. It was begun forty years ago, and it is hardly creditable that in 1863 it had progressed but a short way. The Civil War caused a long suspension of the work, but within the last few years it has progressed with speed. It is now (I believe) about 400 feet high, but it is to be considerably higher. Its design is very simple but impressive—a great square column gradually tapering, made of immense blocks of white marble. It stands in the public park, and although not on very high ground, it presents itself to notice in all directions and at very long distances from the city.

On the opposite bank of the Potomac is the city of Alexandria, to which I refer only to say that from the steamboat you get an excellent view of Washington, sloping gradually up the river bank, and very fair to see in the bright warm glow of this October evening.

From Baltimore south the number of the negroes increases in a marked manner, and here in Washington there is a large population of them. I wish to say of this long-oppressed race that, so far as I can judge, they are playing their part in life, on the whole, well and creditably. I speak of what I have myself seen. All over the country, in the Pullman sleepers, they act as porters, rarely as conductors; though I have thought at times that many of them were superior to their superiors. In many places—San Francisco, for instance—they monopolise the waiting to a great extent. They are rising certainly, but rising slowly in the social scale. Nor is this to be wondered at, for it must be admitted that they are looked upon with disfavour even by many who were advocates for their enfranchisement. It is difficult to get whites to work harmoniously with them, and for this physical reasons are sometimes put forward.

I am told that the negroes farther south are not like the negroes I have seen, that the former show no trace of improvement from the old days when their masters owned them. Of this I cannot speak, but I must say I have found them north, west and east, good-natured, patient, fairly intelligent, and, when properly approached, quite anxious to be obliging. I must speak of one in particular, my friend Joe Green, who is a kind of factotum and a very valuable one, too, for Mr. Frank Thomson on board his railway car. Joe is porter, conductor, cook, courier, and valet, all rolled into one; and he is excellent in each capacity, and in all. In a word, I know no white man in his rank of life who could, in racing parlance, give an ounce to Joe Green over any intelligent course. Full bred.

The grown negroes are not beautiful to look at, but they are well-built generally and the little pickaninnies are really often very pretty, with their curly black heads, funny rolling eyes, and pearly white teeth. I am sure May and Bertie, Lily and Margaret would be delighted with them.

There is a considerable Irish population in Washington, and an informant whom I believe to be reliable told me that between them and the Germans the greater part of the real estate of the city is engrossed.

Of one man, a county Armagh man, born near Belleek, not far from Newry in the direction of Newtown Hamilton, I must speak. He is typical, in some respects at least, of many of his countrymen in America. They have several children. One is a lawyer and newspaper editor in, I think, Arizona. The younger ones are learning trades, or are becoming well-educated. He insisted on my walking with him to his house, where there were assembled some friends from Philadelphia to celebrate his silver wedding. [By the by, it is time to think of celebrating another silver wedding!] At his house, in every way comfortable, he got his youngest child, aged about nine— a girl—to play some Irish airs, which she did fairly well.

We talked over his own history and incidentally of politics.

He fought for the North all through the war and has now buried somewhere in his chest a bullet which the surgeons cannot get at and which occasionally troubles him. He is now a clerk in a Government department at Washington.

He is a Democrat in American politics and firmly

believes (as I find a good many more do also) not only that General McClellan was the great soldier of the North, but also that, if he had been loyally supported at the beginning, he would have made short work of it. He believes that, because he (McClellan) was a Democrat, the Republicans in power were unwilling that he should have too much glory; for they knew that that meant the advent of the Democrats to power and McClellan for President. As to home politics, he is, like all the Easterners, with few exceptions whom we met, an advanced Nationalist. Any man who, by any means almost short of murder and dynamite, would try to help Ireland, and (which is often thought to be the same thing) flout England and England's statesmen, has his best sympathies. He is inclined to think Parnell too moderate. He is a diligent reader of the "Irish World," published by a Mr. Patrick Ford, which I have only twice seen, but which I find is a real power amongst the Irish here. They believe in Mr. Ford's honesty; and they know it means ill to England and believe it means well to Ireland. There is no journalist in America who to so large an extent can influence the pockets and the political action of the Irish in America.

Kilmartin is another Irishman, in America almost from boyhood, who learned his trade of blacksmith here, and who is now a master of his craft with men in his employment. He is as ardent a politician as the other, and heartily devoted to the old Faith. He was spending Sunday in visiting the neighbourhood of Alexandria, where two of his children are at Catholic boarding-schools. I find that on the whole the influence of Catholic priests is great in America amongst Catholics, but nothing compared with what it is, or rather with what it was, years ago in Ireland. This lessened influence by no means necessarily implies lessened religious devotion. In truth to the evil policy, in bygone times, of England, the priesthood in Ireland owed much of their influence. Who was there to "stand up to" the local landlord but the priest? Who to vindicate public rights against private oppression but the priest? And when the law gave the franchise to the peasant-serf, but enjoined that it should be exercised under the eye of agent and bailiff, who but the priest was bold enough to tell the people that in their union they could defy landlord tyranny? Who but the priest with voice loud enough to reach them, to tell them that the right exercise of the franchise was a matter not of caprice or private interest, but public duty? I do not refer to those times still further back when law made the persecuted, spy-hunted priest an object of deepest love and highest veneration.

With altered conditions—better laws in Ireland, with the gradually growing independence and strength and intelligence of the people, it is in the nature of things that the priest should keep more and more within the sanctuary and mix less and less in secular affairs, and even in political affairs, save where these seem to affect some moral interests.

On this point it is curious and interesting to note the altered tone of a portion of the English press. Time was when it was confidently said—undo, undermine the influence of the Catholic priest: take education wholly from his control; free the Irish people from the spiritual thraldom which they suffer, and the Anglo-Irish difficulty will speedily come to an end.

Well—what do these same scribes say now? I will not stop to give the answer.

I have had a very long tramp to-day and a long scribble, and exhausted nature cries out, "Spare yourself and your devoted family for the present." Amen, I sleepily respond.

MONDAY, OCT. 8, 1883.
(Washington and *en route* for New York)

To-day we continued our peregrination. I will say nothing of the art and scientific collection beyond this, that Corcoran's (due to the munificent endowment of a banker of that name) Art Gallery has many notable objects, amongst them Power's famous "Greek Slave," and that the Smithsonian Museum (also due to private munificence) is rich in objects of interest in natural history, and especially relating to early America.

The White House (the President's residence) is a fine, roomy, plain, sensible gentleman's residence on a large scale—nothing more. President Arthur was in New York, but the gates were open; and, whether the President be there or not, the people are free to come and go as far as the grounds are concerned. There is no pretentious fuss about, and no soldier or policeman was, or generally is, in attendance.

The Capitol, of which Washington himself laid the foundation stone, is a building of which Americans are proud and with reason. It comprises the Senate House, the House of Representatives, the Congressional Library, and the Court, in which the Supreme Court of Appeal of the United States sits.

I could, I should think, mention several public buildings which in some particulars I should prefer to the Capitol; but, taking it as a whole, its *situs,* its general effect, its suitability for all allotted purposes, and the practical common-sense brought to bear in carrying out these purposes, I cannot name any one building of a similar nature which, I think, is equal to it.

I won't describe its parts in detail. The House of Representatives is adorned with fine portraits of La-fayette and Washington; and I notice in the outer lobby several large paintings of greater or less artistic merit, one-half of them perpetuating incidents of the great war of the Revolution and England's defeated part in them, and perpetuated, I need hardly say, purely from the American standpoint.

The House of Representatives is larger, a good

deal larger, than the English House of Commons, and its arrangements take greater care of the physical comfort of its members. Each member has a comfortable chair with a convenient writing desk in front of him. Contrast this with the scramble for seats in the Commons, with its absence of all writing or note-taking conveniences and the difference is striking, and oh! the misery for the first time of rising with only the bare back of a bench before you.

There is, it seems, no recognised place for Republicans and Democrats, or for government and non-government men. There is a general ballot, but by exchange and mutual concession men get settled down amongst those with whom they usually act, as with us.

This is not the place in which to stop to notice the extraordinary fact that in the American system of political government the Cabinet of the President are not seated in the legislative chambers to propound or to defend the policy of the Government of the day. But it is a curious political fact.

I regretted we were obliged to leave Washington so soon, though I believe we pretty well exhausted its objects of interest. Between Washington and Philadelphia the journey is through a country interesting in itself, and interesting because full of incidents relating to the two great struggles in which young America has so far been engaged. Between Washington and New York, indeed, the whole country is interesting and picturesque, numbers of rivers which anywhere else would deserve to be called great rivers, again and again appearing. Between the points last named we touch or cross the Potomac, the Gunpowder, the Bush, the Susquehanna (which discharges into Chesapeake Bay), the Delaware and the Passaic rivers amongst others. I will not stop to describe them; but the Susquehanna looked especially lovely where we crossed it, the town of Havre-de-Grace being on one side and Ferryville on the other.

At Philadelphia we were joined by Mr. Thomson and by some of his friends, who, like Mr. Thomson and myself, were to dine at the Knickerbocker Club in the evening—of which more hereafter.

I had hoped to be able to return to Philadelphia later, but to my great regret this was found to be impossible.

Philadelphia is in population the second city in the States, while in the area it covers and in the number of its buildings it comes first. It has historic interest, too—for it was here in 1776 that the Declaration of Independence was signed and published. By the way, I learned at Washington that Charles Carroll of Carrolton, the only Irishman and Catholic who so far as I know was a signatory to this Declaration, has living descendants held in honour and respect.

From Philadelphia to Jersey City was only at most a two hours' journey by express train, and in the pleasant company in which I found myself it seemed

much less. I must say something of the personnel
of this party. *Imprimis,* Mr. Thomson, not given
to long monologues himself, but following apparently with interest the monologues of other people
and always ready to draw others out. Mr. Rawle, a
Philadelphia lawyer of some eminence—"Rawle on
Covenants"—in fact, gentlemanly, quiet, and unassuming. Mr. MacVeagh is a lawyer of note. He
was Attorney-General of the States during poor
President Garfield's short reign. He, although an
Irishman by parentage, is to my eye in some respects
more like the typical Yankee in physique than many
whom I have met. In manner his descent is betrayed.
He interested me very much—a lean, colourless, wiry
man, distinctly bilious-looking. He is vehement, eloquent, humorous, and apparently greatly in earnest
about every topic which cropped up big and little.
He is a Republican in politics, but (as I gathered)
had kicked over the traces; is anything but a docile
man in the hands of the wire-pullers, and altogether
the kind of man who has views and ideas of his own
which greatly detract from his value as a steady-go-
ing, thick-and-thin party adherent. And there are
men, even in politics, to be found to admire such men!

The only unmentioned one of our party was Senator Bayard—Democrat Senator for the State of Delaware, or, to speak in more constitutional language,
returned for that State. He is a big, jolly, good-
looking man with indications of power about his

rather massive head and face. A political opponent, but admirer of his, afterwards told me "If Bayard were nominated by the Democrats, he would be President to a certainty."

"How is that?"

"Well, he is a fairly able man, and he is more than a fairly honest man."

"Will he get the Democratic nomination?"

"No chance, I think, but I don't know."

"Why?"

"Well, I guess he is too honest for his party. They would want to stipulate with him that he would turn out neck and crop all the Republicans in office. They want all the loaves and fishes for themselves—all, big and little. Now Senator Bayard, I guess, would go a long way to meet views but not that length."

I played the part of listener with interest and amusement and soon we found ourselves at Jersey City.

I prefer listening in American conversation and for several reasons. You learn more by holding your tongue unless indeed you open it to ask questions. But more, the conversation is more or less of an effort. Very frequently American gentlemen "orate" where we should talk in conversation loosely and without any very close attention to our parts.

The dinner at the Knickerbocker was pleasant and good—our host, Mr. C. Randolph Robinson, whom you will recollect in Harley Street—a leading New

York lawyer and an amiable, gentlemanly man. He might not take it for a compliment, and I mean merely to say what I think, when I add that he is very like in manner what a good type of man at the Bar with us is. Lord Coleridge, Lord Justice Bowen, and myself were the only foreigners present. Amongst the notables was the head of the house of Astor, the largest real estate owners in the city and whose wealth is said to be enormous. He seemed a quiet, unassuming man who made no large contribution to the stock of talk. Mr. Evarts was also here, pleasant, witty, and as unserious on serious topics as ever. His partner, Mr. Choate, too—a man of considerable reputation. By the way, what a relief it would be to have that partnership system at the Bar with us. I feel I have now got to that time of life when I could lend the dignity of my name, such as it is, and the benefit of a general supervising experience to an efficient partner who should be allowed to earn all the money (sharing it with me) and also to enjoy all the honour and glory!

My neighbour was a benevolent, chubby, and interesting man, Mr. John Jay, formerly a lawyer, and grandson of the first Chief Justice of the United States.

The Chief Justice was (with Franklin and others), one of the American representatives in the peace negotiations and stoutly resisted the advice of Franklin to rely on the guidance and counsels of France, which the Chief Justice thoroughly distrusted. Mr. Jay is delighted to find that only quite recently the laborious researches of Mr. Lecky have thoroughly vindicated his distinguished ancestor's wisdom and conduct.

The only remaining guest I need mention is my friend, Mr. Cadwalader, also a lawyer of distinction of New York, to whose kind hospitality and attention much of the pleasure of my visit to America is due. You will have noticed how many of the people whose names I introduce belong to the profession of the law. No doubt "birds of a feather flock together"; but the fact is that lawyers are about the most numerous professional class in the country, and they have managed to secure a larger share in the government of their country in important places than probably any two other classes together. I propose to treat you hereafter to some general observations upon some special points of interest which have struck me, and I shall again recur to this topic.

The evening passed very enjoyably, but I must admit the conversation had occasionally more of effort and less of careless spontaneity than with us. "Oh," said one of my friends in answer to my observation, "it isn't merely that they orate, they perorate"; anyway, they cannot be accused of what our distinguished conversationalists, including Macaulay the brilliant, were said habitually to do—namely, prepare their topics *a priori* and get some ingenious friend to lead up to their carefully prepared impromptus. By the way I find the Chief Justice of England has acquired quite a reputation as a raconteur. He certainly has no end of stories which he is always willing to let off pleasantly upon very slight provocation in whatever company he chances to find himself.

TUESDAY, OCT. 9, 1883.
(At New York)

AFTER the many discomforts inseparable from prolonged and rapid travelling I am glad to find myself at the Hotel Brunswick once more in comfortable if not luxurious quarters. New York is to me what Capua was to Hannibal's soldiers, but it will not, I hope, have the same enervating effects.

I had noticed in the papers in the west several times that I was to be asked to lead in the defence of O'Donnell, but, not finding any despatches on the subject on my arrival here, I had begun to hope there was nothing in the rumour. The case seems a desperate one, and besides, as you know, criminal cases are very wide of my line. This morning, however, a gentleman waited upon me (Mr. Moran, I think was his name) who said he was connected with the legal profession and also (as I understood him) connected with the "Irish World," which has been instrumental in collecting funds for O'Donnell's defence. I told him I had heard nothing from England about the matter;

that the case was out of my ordinary line of practice;
that Mr. Sullivan could thoroughly well do all that
it was possible to do in such a case, and that I could
say nothing definite about the matter until I reached
England, except this, that personally I should much
prefer not to be in the case, but that I should not feel
justified professionally in declining to act if my services were desired by the prisoner's friends. In short,
I did not like the case, but would not shirk the responsibility.

I own to the fear that it may be desired to conduct
the defence upon lines not wholly conceived with a
view to saving O'Donnell's life. Against this, if I
have anything to do with the case, I shall steadfastly
set my face.

I went to lunch at the Windsor with Lord Justice
Bowen and Lord Carington, Lord Coleridge and his
son. Major Baring also lunched there. We had a
very cheery party. The Chief Justice was in great
spirits and has obviously enjoyed his trips to Chicago,
St. Louis, and elsewhere. He has had to do a good
deal of talking, or as they frequently call it here, chin-
music. The appetite of the Americans for oratory
seems to me insatiable. In this respect they beat the
Irish hollow. I have seen them sit through hours of
oratory—good, bad, and indifferent, and show no
signs of impatience. He dined at a so-called private
dinner party in Chicago, at which he was assured no
press man would be present, but was horrified to hear

his host informed that copies of his (the host's) speech of the evening had been duly forwarded to the local papers. In the result the speeches lasted till the small hours of the morning, and the Chief Justice had the satisfaction of seeing the host's speech, full of wit and epigram, carefully and literally reported!

This Windsor Hotel is one of the finest, if not the finest, in New York. The best hotels here are certainly dearer than the best with us—for instance, Lord Carington paid for a small sitting-room and a bedroom seventeen dollars a day, covering bed and board. At the Brunswick the charge for a small bedroom with a bath annexed is from five dollars per day, for rooms alone.

In the evening Martin and I dined together quietly and afterwards went to the Madison Square Theatre and saw a piece called "The Rajah." Neither play nor players were remarkable. By the way, the usual mode of spelling "theater" and "center" are as I have here written them down. Traveller and travelling are almost invariably spelt with one "l."

NEW YORK, WEDNESDAY, OCT. 10, 1883.

THIS was comparatively a quiet day. The morning I spent walking about the streets, which remind me more of Paris than of any other place.

In the afternoon I went with my friend Mr. E. L. Godkin, partly by the elevated railway and partly by carriage, to the gentlemen's driving park, Fleetwood, to see some good trotting. This elevated railway is, so far as I know, a perfectly unique institution. It traverses the city practically from end to end, running through, or to be more correct, running *above* some of the most busy thoroughfares at an elevation of (speaking roughly) fifty to one hundred and fifty feet. It extends beyond the Central Park, and near this its elevation is greatest. Standing upon what in the distance seems very slight scaffolding, and seen from a low standpoint against the warm evening sky, the appearance of the train speeding along as it were in mid-air is very startling. So far as I can gather no compensation was paid to the owners of property in the streets along which the railway runs, although in many cases the real damage done must have been considerable. The number of passengers carried by it must be something enormous. For ten cents you can journey its entire length; and for five cents you can go the full length of any of the stages or tram railways. Moving about the city by these means is one of the few cheap things in America. But, if you come to use a one-horse or two-horse carriage the charges are about double or treble our ordinary cab fares, but you get a much more respectable looking article.

The trotting drive at Fleetwood, which is club property, is a circular measured mile in circumference, with a members' stand and enclosure, and also with one open to the public on payment. This trotting

seems a passion with New York gentlemen, and I
think Mr. W. H. Vanderbilt would hear with greater
equanimity of the failure of a great *coup* in Wall
Street than he would that Mr. Work had a newly-ac-
quired team which would beat hollow the record of
his famous trotters, Maud S. and Aline.

Several of the men and of the horses famous in
trotting circles were here. Mr. Work and his famous
team, **Swiveller** and Edward; **Mr.** Shepperd F.
Knapp and a pair of very promising youngsters; and
Mr. W. K. Vanderbilt, but neither Maud S. nor Aline
was here. The main feature of the day's sport was a
race among the members driving their own teams in
ordinary trotting wagons with the restriction that the
horses competing should not previously have exceeded
a certain time record, as, for instance, a mile in 2.40
or 2.50. The false starts were the principal interest
in the race. There were some nine competitors, and,
as a flying start is permitted, the difficulty is to get
them at the right moment on equitable terms.

Of much more interest to me was the speeding of
Mr. Work's crack team round the course under the
guidance of a crack driver, John Murphy. I said
to Mr. Knapp, "Is he a good man at this work?"

"About the best we have and honest as steel."

Murphy seemed quite a popular hero, very much
after the manner of Archer, Fordham, John Osborn,
and Cannon with us. Murphy is a man of about
forty, a lithe, spare frame, good, broad shoulders,

and a determined face. Off they go for a breather round the track; and, as they come round the home-stretch, they are going at a capital pace; and, nearing the starting-point, John Murphy is seen to nod to the gentlemen in the Judges' stand; and, as the team dash past, the official stop watches (and hundreds besides) are set to check the record. "They will do the mile in a shade under 2.20," said Mr. Work, to whose kindness I was indebted for this treat.

On they went at what seemed to me a terrific pace, sending up a cloud of sand and dust which rendered quite necessary the protective goggles with which the driver was adorned. As they came closer to us, the speed seemed even greater; and, as they were rounding for the home stretch, Mr. Work's quick eye detected something wrong. "By gad, Edward has broke. Well, I would have laid a thousand dollar note against that something has happened." Before the sentence is well finished, the horses have swept by, and a thousand watches are consulted, and presently the official record is prominently displayed, showing that the gallant chestnut and bay, have sped their mile in 2 min. 19¾ sec. Mr. Work was right. Something had happened. Edward had struck and slightly cut the heel of his near forefoot, which had caused him, usually as steady as a rock, to break his trot.

Mr. Work's stables are very perfect and complete. Their kindly owner devotes a great deal of time, and takes a great deal of interest in this favourite Ameri-

can pastime, and it was, I fear, a bitter moment for
him when he learned that Mr. W. K. Vanderbilt with
Maud S. and Aline had beaten the best record of his
crack team. It is not without interest to note how the
best record keeps constantly being beaten. Fifteen
years ago a mile in 2.40 for a single horse was considered a tip-top performance. To-day Jay Eye See
trotted a mile in 2.10½, and a horse called Johnstone,
the property of Mr. Case, paced a mile in even less
time the other day at Chicago.

My friend Mr. Godkin and Holmes dined with me
at Delmonico's in Fifth Avenue, where we had an excellent dinner and at a cost by no means extravagant,
considering the reputation of the restaurant.

Later we went to the Star Theatre to see the trag-
edy of "Francesca da Rimini," written by quite a
modern playwright. You know the story. I cannot
say I greatly enjoyed the piece. It was too doleful,
but unquestionably Barrett played the part of the de-
formed Gianciotto with considerable power and dignity.

NEW YORK, THURSDAY, OCT. 11, 1883.

I SPENT the early day rambling about alone and
pleasantly enough. I find the people quite civil,
as civil if not as polite as the Parisian in the days of
the Empire, and certainly much more civil than the
general run of Englishmen. I do not want, by the
way, to be taken for a Bonapartist, but have you not

noticed that, since the Empire suddenly crumpled up, the manners of the people of Paris have retrograded? It seems to me their civility to men and their deference to women are not what they once were. Here I am struck with the marked deference paid to women. They give place to them in the streets, in the railways, and in the stage cars in a way quite nice to see. Women, too, of all classes and ages, go about in the public streets and in the public conveyances, too, alone in a way quite unknown to us. I suppose there are exceptions to the rule, but here they do not seem to suffer from the annoyance which one hears frequently spoken of in London and other cities. I dined with my friend Mr. Cadwalader at his luxurious bachelor quarters in 35th St., where I met in addition to my friends Mr. Frank Thomson and Mr. E. R. Robinson, of whom I have already spoken more than once, Mr. Carter and Mr. Parsons (two lawyers eminent in this city) and Mr. Justice Lawrence, a Judge of the Supreme Court. A most pleasant and enjoyable evening it was, and I regretted being obliged to cut it short in order to attend the great Coleridge function fixed to take place to-night.

I am struck with the candour with which men here discuss their institutions political, religious, and social, and admit generally with great frankness the blots in the existing condition of things. But I need hardly add they still claim to be the greatest and most powerful nation this world has yet seen; and they even point exultingly to their very weaknesses as proofs of their glory and their greatness; for what but a country of great resources (mental, moral, and material) could be great and glorious in spite of these drawbacks?

The great function to which I have alluded is the reception to-night of Lord Coleridge at the Academy of Music by the Bar Association of the State of New York. The first of these associations in the State in point of time as well as influence and importance, is the Bar Association of the City of New York. This association will do honour to Lord Coleridge at a later date, and a number of its members took part in to-night's affair; but on the whole, for reasons to which reference here need not be made, they have not acted cordially with the State Association, which has been actively represented by Mr. Elliott F. Shepard, the attentive host of Lord Coleridge up to this time.

The history of the City Association is in the highest degree creditable to the members of the legal profession in New York. It sprang into existence during what is still called the infamous Tweed régime, when corruption stalked all-powerful, and when what was called justice was by some of its administrators an article sold to the highest bidder. It was then that the best men at the Bar banded themselves together and finally succeeded in hurling with infamy from the Bench two of the men who had most disgraced it—I mean Judge Barnard and Judge Cardozo. I have no doubt that many of my friends at the English Bar have had before them (as I have had) some of the remarkable decisions of Judge Barnard in relation to the Erie Railway Company.

The Academy of Music, which is, in fact, the Opera House, was very well filled throughout. Towards the front of the stage was erected a platform, on which was seated Chief Justice Ruger of the State of New York, and other distinguished members of the reception committee, with, of course, the guest of the evening. This platform was the only thing that detracted from the striking character of the scene, but it really fitted in very badly, not to say ludicrously, with the surroundings. It was narrow, without railings, and rose boldly and abruptly from the stage; and upon it were huddled together, on chairs perilously close to the precipitous edges of the platform, a number of gentlemen, generally speaking, old and bald-headed, and also (I need not add) eminent and respectable. This platform was a mistake. One trembled for the fate of many if only one were indiscreet.

The proceedings began by a speech pitched in a high key of righteousness, delivered by Mr. Elliott F. Shepard, wherein he introduced the Chief Justice of England to the Chief Justice Ruger. Next followed a speech by Chief Justice Ruger, a speech of honest welcome to their distinguished guest. I confess to liking Chief Justice Ruger's speech, for it was direct to its purpose, and, if commonplace in manner and matter, was real and unaffected.

My good friend Mr. Evarts followed. He seems to me to be indispensable in these matters and commonly fills the rôle of "great orator of the day." Of Mr. Evarts' speech it is enough to say that he probably could not make a bad speech if he tried; and so on the present occasion there were clever touches of humour and deft involutions of phraseology which tickled the ear if they did not yield much food to the mental palate. He was supposed to represent the professional element in the welcome. There was perhaps in this relation more humour than judgment shown in his emphasising the fact that, while lawyers were accused of fleecing their clients, they never flayed them, and that a judicious amount of fleecing was supposed to add to the quantity and improve the quality of the wool.

Then followed Lord Coleridge, who was warmly received. His commanding figure and perfectly modulated voice soon arrested and kept the attention of his audience. I am not going to say that this was in any sense a great speech or that it contained a compendium of political or any other wisdom. In point of manner of delivery and as to tone and language, it was Lord Coleridge at his best, and that is saying a great deal; but it was after all a speech of an occasion (as the French say) into which it would have been extremely difficult, even if it had been wise, to say anything at once profound and acceptable about American institutions and conditions of things. His speech for the time and place and occasion was admirable. It was not unqualified praise, and it was not carping censure. He praised with discrimination, and he censured in a way to impart to his praise a flavour of judicial impartiality. As was once said of Townsend and the House of Commons, "he fairly hit his audience 'twixt wind and water." So far as one can judge, his speech has been uncommonly well received throughout the country. The statement which perhaps for readers at home has the most interest is that in which he said that, though he admired Mr. Gladstone much and was a steady supporter of his government, yet that John Bright was the man with whose political sentiments he (Lord Coleridge) most frequently found himself in accord. If this were designed as a rhetorical artifice to catch his audience, it was very clever and very successful. Richard Cobden was a great English name, almost the only great English name, with the American people, but amongst living men John Bright's is the only one to conjure with on the American continent. It is to be noted, however, that this profession of radical faith comes at the time when John Bright's radicalism has passed its apogee, and his views are in some respects at least supposed to be narrow and reactionary. I thought, as I walked home after this brilliant gathering, "I suppose Lord Coleridge does not forget that

JOHN MITCHEL

amongst one of John Bright's most famous public ut-
terances not yet recalled, was one in which he maintained that an hereditary legislative chamber could
not be permanently maintained in a free State."

FRIDAY, OCT. 12, 1883.

I VISITED Castle Garden to-day, a spot full of interest to all who follow the fortunes of the emi-
grant, for it is here that he first sets foot on American soil, and he is enrolled with careful particulars
amongst the inhabitants of the country. I reserve,
however, a full description of the place until I shall
have paid another and longer visit. I was anxious to
see the widow of poor John Mitchel, of "The United
Irishmen" and the "Jail Journal." My interest in
Mrs. Mitchel dates a long way back. She is the
daughter of a Captain Verner (one of the family of
Co. Armagh Verners). He was a tenant of my
father in Ballybot, Newry, and it was while living
here (next door indeed to our old family house, where
all of us children were born) that she eloped with
John Mitchel, then, I think, practising as a Solicitor,
and one of the firm of Frazer and Mitchel. Poor
Mrs. Mitchel! To look at, she was always weak and
fragile, and yet she has shown more than once in her
life that she has great nerve and resolution. It must
have been very soon after her marriage that John
Mitchel became prominent in Dublin as a politician

and a journalist. Many have been found to condemn
what they considered the wickedness or impolicy of
his political course, but no one has questioned his sin-
gle-mindedness and honesty of purpose. The only
time I ever recollect seeing him was when the railway
from Dublin reached no farther north than Drog-
heda. We were both going to Dublin, and both got
on the coach together on the Ballybot side of the town
close to Turner's Glen. He was a man not easily for-
gotten, and his conversation and appearance made a
deep impression upon the little lad, his fellow-trav-
eller, that day. I well recollect his dark straight
hair, almost whiskerless face, and sallow, colourless,
bloodless complexion, which, combined with a certain sharpness of feature and nobility of brow, gave
him a peculiarly intellectual appearance, with a look
almost of the ascetic. The square character of his
jaw and the firmness of his mouth conveyed the
notion of a resolute, not to say obstinate, man; a
notion which was not removed by the look of his
dark grey eyes, which seemed full of dreams and
melancholy.

I still think him the most brilliant journalistic
writer I have ever known. He had not perhaps the
breadth of Frederick Lucas, nor the wide information
of Gavan Duffy, nor the tender pathetic imagination
of Thomas Davis; but his style was more terse, vigorous, and to the point than theirs and was wholly
free from affectation of scholarship foreign to the

matter in hand. Occasionally in a sentence he could condense a world of argument. One instance occurs to me. In one of a series of letters addressed to the Orangemen of the North, he is pointing out to them why they should be in the van of the National movement, as their fathers had been in 1782 and 1798; and he is meeting an objection supposed to be made by an Orangeman then, and certainly frequently made for him since, namely: that to join with the Irish papist would be to join the children of Antichrist, and so on. Each July 12th celebration makes one familiar with this kind of thing. John Mitchel did not proceed gravely to argue that, after all, the evidence was not quite conclusive that the Pope was really Antichrist, and that, after all, all Irishmen, even Irish papists, were bound up with the weal or woe of their country. He did none of these things. In the language of the now defunct special pleader he put in a plea of confession and avoidance. He wrote a single line. "The Pope may be Antichrist, but, Orangemen of the North, he serves no ejectments in Ulster."

His second son, James Mitchel[1] (his only surviving son), a little resembles his father in the placid expression of his face, in his voice, and in his absence of colour. He has not the strong masterful expres-

---

[1] He died in 1908, and in the Catholic Faith, which at least two of his sisters had adopted—without any opposition from their father, who once told John O'Hagan that, if he could pray, he would become a Catholic.

sion of his father. That he is as advanced a politician on Irish affairs as his father a chance expression revealed. I said, "You, I think, take no part in politics." "No, since the war I have had nothing to do in any way with politics." Later on in our conversation the name of John Dillon came up. "Yes," said he, "he is thoroughly honest, but he is too moderate a politician for my taste." "Well, this is the first time I have heard John Dillon called a moderate politician," I answered, laughing heartily; and so ended our conversation.

I found Mrs. Mitchel looking stronger and stouter than I had ever before seen her. Trouble had indeed silvered her head, but, considering the sorrows which have been crowded into her life, she seemed in good spirits. To look at her you would hardly imagine that, friendless, she ran the blockade to join her husband and sons in the South.

You will recollect that in the War of Secession here John Mitchel took part with the South, not, I am persuaded, because of his love of the institution of slavery, but because he believed in the right of the Southern States to govern themselves. I speak here of what I may call the natural right of the South. There is probably little doubt that as to the matter of legal right the weight of legal authority was with the South.

As in whatever he attempted, John Mitchel was never half hearted in his support; so he risked every-

thing, person, position, means, and (more precious
than all these) his three sons for the cause he
espoused.

It is a very sad story. The eldest son displayed
considerable military genius, and was in command of
Fort Sumter when a chance cannon-ball ended a life
full of great promise. The third died on the field of
battle; and the second son, James, of whom I have
spoken, more than once wounded in actual conflict, alone survives, carrying with him as he will
to the end the maiming and disfiguring marks of
war.

With Mrs. Mitchel in all her troubles this consol-
ing thought may abide, that, however men may differ
as to John Mitchel's conduct, measured by the cold
standard of prudence, all men recognise in him the
rare stuff of sterling, unselfish devotion to the cause
he advocated.

I dined in the evening with Mr. E. L. Godkin at
25th St., a very pleasant gathering.

SATURDAY, OCT. 13, 1883.

M Y friend Mr. E. R. Robinson drove me to-day
to Jerome Park to see some American flat racing. We went along the Hudson side of the Park at
first by what is called the Riverside Road, and afterwards by the road known as the Grand Boulevard.
The glimpses of the Hudson River and of the Pali-

sades on the opposite side of the river were very beautiful.

These two very fine roads are due to the Tweed régime period. They are very fine wide roads, worthy of what I feel certain will be the future of this suburb. New York is probably not the only city in the world which owes its adornment to a profligate administration. The fact is a great deal of work done in Tweed's time was conceived in a worthy spirit, but the municipality was made to pay three or four prices for it. It is, I believe, computed that Tweed brought the municipality into debt to the amount of fifty million dollars, for which value was received to the extent of about fifteen millions. At present the tide of fashion following the line of Fifth Avenue is distinctly setting towards the other and lower side of the Park. I shall be disappointed if this continues. When next I visit New York (and I hope I shall be able to do that before ten years are over) I expect to find this riverside district with proper road approaches and other means of access; and I shall be disappointed if the millionaires are not there, disputing for sites in this picturesque neighbourhood. The fact is Fifth Avenue is too narrow for a great fashionable centre, and in a few years it will probably be found to contain (at least to a great extent) business houses.

Jerome Park is named after the gentleman who owns the soil, and who is, I believe, the father-in-law of Lord Randolph Churchill. It is leased and managed by a club very much on the principle of the Sandown Park near London; but the racing track, as it is called, is not nearly so good as that of the latter. It is a pretty enough place, and an evening can be very pleasantly passed there; but it is not racing one sees.

The track is too confined, the curves are too sharp, and the straight run is too short (only about two furlongs) to allow a really good horse to get fully into his stride. They have a very sensible plan here. The bookmakers, or professional betting-men, they confine to a particular spot away from the main stands; and they make them pay a very considerable sum for liberty to bet. This serves two useful purposes. It enables the authorities to exercise surveillance as to the character and stability of the professional betting-men, and also is a sensible mode of compelling that class, who alone in the long run make money by race-betting, to contribute to the endowment of racing. It is notorious in England that thousands of acres and many thousands of pounds, nay, many great fortunes, are being swallowed up by the bookmakers in every decade of years, and yet these gentry pay on the same principle as the general public, at whose cost they wear purple and fine linen and feast sumptuously every day.

In the evening I assisted at a grand dinner given by my friend Mr. Evarts. Sir James Hannen, Sir Ar-

thur Hobhouse, and myself were the only foreigners.
The company was principally made up of lawyers and
judges with a few civilians thrown in.

It was a bright, cheery, and in every way pleasant
party, and it was late before we left the steps of our
entertaining host.

APPENDIX

BY THOMAS F. MEEHAN, A.M.

GREÀTLY as he marveled at all he saw in the Northwest during his trip in 1883, one can not help thinking how much greater would be his amazement could Lord Russell return and make the same trip to-day. The Alaska-Yukon-Pacific Exposition of the summer of 1909, at Seattle, drew the attention of the people of the United States specially to the wonders and progress of the Pacific Coast.

At the inaugural ceremonies of the Seattle Exposition James J. Hill, the great railroad magnate of the Northwest, forcefully insisted on the fact that the growth resulting from the building of new railways is similar to that produced by the introduction of irrigation. A survey of conditions presented to-day at the points mentioned in Lord Russell's diary, and those he found there during his journey in 1883, will aptly serve as a confirmation of this statement.

Admitted to the Federal Union on November 11, 1889, the great agricultural State of Washington has developed out of the then fallow Territory, and keeping pace with its marvelous industrial and commercial expansion we find Oregon and Idaho. Spokane, a city of more than 60,000 inhabitants, where eight railroads enter, in 1880 was but an Indian trading post round which less than 400 people clustered.

The completion of the Northern Pacific gave it new life and started it on the road to its present prosperity. Tacoma, then almost unknown, is a great manufacturing and industrial city of 110,000 inhabitants.

Seattle is a metropolis built in a generation. In 1880 it included within its limited area 3,533 people; in 1890, 42,837; in 1900, 80,000; and to-day probably it has 250,000. Four transcontinental railroads make it a huge forwarder of freights and the centre of an enormous trade to Japan and the East. Its harbor, Elliott Bay, has become a leading ocean port, where the whole American fleet could anchor.

In 1904 on its banks the battleship *Nebraska* was launched. Built originally on a hill, modern engineering is accomplishing one of its most astounding feats in changing the grade of the city's twenty-one miles of streets. To level the hill and make convenient ways for traffic, fourteen million cubic yards of earth have to be moved, with a maximum cut of one hundred and twenty feet, and a minimum fill of fifty-four feet, a process which, it is claimed, involves the carriage of more ground than any other modern undertaking except the Panama Canal. The tide flats of thirty years ago have been filled in and are now the heart of the business district, covered with railroad terminals, factories, and warehouses. Intellectual life has also quickened and expanded along all the lines of progressive citizenship.

Magnificent as has all this material development proved, it in no sense exceeds what has been accomplished by the Church throughout the same territory, during the period that has elapsed since 1883. The figures presented by the Catholic statistics to-day, in comparison with those of 1883, are as notable as any of those in the commercial or industrial expansion. When Lord Russell visited this section Washington Territory comprised the Diocese of Nesqually, established May 31, 1850, as a suffragan of the Province of Oregon, which included besides Oregon, Idaho, Vancouver Island, and Alaska. The Metropolitan was the martyr Archbishop Charles J. Seghers, who was assassinated by a degenerate half-breed on November 28, 1886. Bishop Ægidius Junger, who died December 26, 1889, presided over Nesqually, and had his Cathedral at Vancouver. Under his jurisdiction were about 25 priests, who attended 30 churches and 64 stations. Seattle, Tacoma, and Spokane had one church each. Schools and institutions under Catholic management were almost unknown outside Vancouver.

The name of the diocese and its see were changed to Seattle September 11, 1907, and it now has 131 priests, of whom 52 are members of regular orders and congregations; 169 churches, 157 stations, 67 chapels; 6 colleges and academies for boys, 18 academies for girls; 13 hospitals; 5 orphan asylums, 5 homes for the poor, and a Catholic population of 85,000.

In addition there have been created the new dioceses of Baker City, 1903; Boise, 1893; Great Falls,

Montana, 1904; Helena, Montana, 1884, and the Prefecture Apostolic of Alaska, 1894. Within their jurisdiction are 100,000 Catholics, 135 priests, and 180 churches.

Idaho in 1883 had 10 priests and churches, and about 3,000 Catholics, of whom more than half were Indians. It was a vicariate and the priests Jesuit missionaries. Dakota was also a vicariate with 36 priests and about 50 churches. It now has four dioceses, Fargo, 1889; Lead, 1892; Sioux Falls, 1896, and Bismarck, 1910. Here there are 133,000 Catholics, 222 priests, and 202 churches.

Councillors

Hon. Edward B. Amend, LL.D.
William R. King
Rev. Thomas J. Campbell, S.J.
Edward J. McGuire, LL.B.
Andrew J. Shipman, LL.B.
Rev. Joseph F. Delany, D.D.

Editing Committee

Charles George Herbermann, LL.D.,
Lit.D., Ph.D.
Rev. Michael J. Considine
Rev. Joseph F. Delany, D.D.
Thomas F. Meehan, A.M.

MEMBERS

Adams, Samuel
Adams, T. Albeus
Adikes, John
Agar, John G.
Ahearn, Jeremiah
Almirall, Raymond F.
Amberg, William A.
Amend, Hon. Edw. B.
Amend, William J.
Amy, Alfred V.
Aspell, Dr. John
Bainton, Dr. Joseph H.
Bartley, Rev. James R.
Baumer, Francis
Bennett, William H.
Benziger, Bruno
Benziger, Louis G.
Benziger, Nicholas C.
Berge, Edward W.
Biersmith, E. L.
Binsse, Henry B.
Bister, John
Blake, Rev. W. L.
Blandford, P. A.
Blenk, Most Rev. James H., D.D.
Bogan, Rev. B. M.
Bonacum, Rt. Rev. Thomas, D.D.
Bornemann, Rev. Geo.
Boylan, Rev. John F.
Brady, Rev. John F.
Brann, Very Rev. Mgr. Henry A., D.D.

Brennan, Alfred T.V.
Brennan, John
Breslin, Rev. P. N.
Briody, Rev. John H.
Bristed, C. A.
Britt, Hon. Philip J.
Broderick, Daniel I.
Brophy, W. H.
Brown, W. J.
Brune, Very Rev. F. J.
Burke, Edmond
Burke, Rev. John J., C.S.P.
Burke, Rt. Rev. Thos. M. A., D.D.
Burtsell, John M.
Burtsell, Very Rev. Mgr. R. L., D.D.
Butler, James
Byrne, Rev. Christopher E.
Byrne, Miss Elizabeth M.
Byrne, James
Byrne, Rt. Rev. W., D.D.
Caffrey, J. J.
Cahalan, John E.
Callahan, Cornelius
Callan, Rev. M. S.
Callanan, L. J.
Campbell, Rev. Jos. C.
Campbell, Rev. Thos. J., S.J.
Carey, Rev. P. P.

CARROLL, JOHN C.
CARROLL, JOHN F.
CARROLL, P. P.
CASEY, A. J.
CHASE, MISS MAUD E.
CHAZAL, LOUIS R.
CHIDWICK, VERY REV. JOHN P.
CHUTE, MRS. S. H.
CLARE, MISS MARY E.
CLARE, WILLIAM F.
CLARK, REV. ARTHUR MARCH
CLARK, WILLIAM B.
CLAUDE, REV. CAPISTRAN, O.M.CAP
COCKRAN, WM. BOURKE
COHALAN, DANIEL F.
COLEMAN, CHAS. W.
COLEMAN, REV. THOS. J.
COLLINS, VERY REV. MGR. CHAS. W.
COLTON, RT. REV. CHAS. H., D.D.
CONATY, RT. REV. THOS. J., D.D.
CONDON, MARTIN
CONDON, PETER
CONNOLLY, REV. ARTHUR T.
CONNOLLY, VERY REV. MGR. JAMES N.
CONROY, CHARLES C.
CONSIDINE, REV. M. J.
COOKE, A. S.
CORLEY, REV. CHARLES R.
COTTER, REV. JAMES H.

COYLE, JOHN J.
COYTE, JAMES SLATER
CRIMMINS, HON. JOHN D.
CRONIN, REV. DANIEL T.
CROSSEY, REV. JOHN J.
CROWNE, J. VINCENT
CULLEN, THOS. F.
CULLUM, REV. HUGH P.
CUNNION, REV. D. C.
CUNNION, FRANK
CUNNION, REV. MALICK A.
CURLEY, T. F.
CURRY, EDWARD J.
CUSACK, RT. REV. THOS. F., D.D.
DALY, DANIEL
DALY, HON. JOSEPH F.
DAVEY, H. J.
DEERY, JOHN J.
DEGOT, MRS. CAMILLE
DEITSCH, MISS
DELANEY, JOHN J.
DELANY, REV. DR. JOS. F.
DELEHANTY, F. B.
DEROO, REV. P.
DEVINE, THOMAS J.
DEVOY, JOHN W.
DIETZ, NICHOLAS
DILLON, REV. FRANCIS J.
DILLON, JOSEPH
DINEEN, REV. JOS. P.
DIXON, ROBERT N.
DOELGER, PETER
DOLLARD, JAMES J.

DONAHUE, RT. REV. P. J., D.D.

DONNELLY, RT. REV. MGR. E. J., V.F.

DONOGHUE, F. X.

DONOHUE, DANIEL

DONOHUE, REV. JOS. P.

DOODY, REV. DANIEL

DOOLEY, M. F.

DOUGHERTY, JAMES E.

DOWLING, AUSTIN

DOWLING, HON. VICTOR J.

DOYLE, ALFRED

DOYLE, JOHN F.

DOYLE, JOHN F., JR.

DRISCOLL, REV. JOHN T.

DRUMMOND, LOUIS E. A.

DRUMMOND, MICHAEL J.

DUCEY, MICHAEL H.

DUFFY, REV. FRANCIS P.

DUFFY, JAMES P. B.

DUFFY, REV. THOS. F.

DUTTON, JOSEPH

DWYER, DR. JOHN

EARLY, REV. TERENCE J.

EDWARDS, RT. REV. MGR. JOHN

EGAN, PETER

EMMET, DR. THOMAS ADDIS

FALAHEE, JOHN J.

FANNING, WILLIAM J.

FARGIS, JOSEPH H.

FARLEY, MOST REV. JOHN M., D.D.

FARLEY, TERENCE

FARRELL, EDWARD D.

FARRELL, REV. HERBERT F.

FARRELLY, STEPHEN

FARRELLY, T. C.

FEEHAN, RT. REV. D. F., D.D.

FEITNER, THOMAS L.

FENLON, JOHN T.

FERRER, DR. JOSÉ M.

FERRIS, JAMES J.

FINLAY, SIDNEY J.

FITZGERALD, HON. JAS. F.

FITZGERALD, REV. THOS. P.

FITZMAURICE, RT. REV. JOHN E., D.D.

FITZPATRICK, REV. MALICK J.

FLANNELLY, REV. JOS. F.

FLOOD, REV. MGR. JAMES J.

FLOYD-JONES, G. STANTON

FOGARTY, THOMAS

FORNES, CHARLES V.

FOX, JOHN

FOX, PATRICK J.

FOY, REV. FRANCIS A.

FRANCISCAN FATHERS

FRANKLIN, JOSEPH

FRAWLEY, HON. JAS. J.

FRAWLEY, REV. JOHN J.

FRIEL, JOHN J.

FULLER, PAUL

GABRIELS, RT. REV. HENRY, D.D.

GANNON, FRANK S.

GARVAN, PATRICK
GASSLER, REV. LEO
GIBBON, JOHN T.
GIBBONS, HIS EMINENCE JAMES CARDINAL
GILLERAN, THOMAS
GLEASON, REV. J. M.
GOESSMANN, MISS HELEN
GOGGIN, REV. JAS. E.
GOODWIN, FRANK J.
GORMAN, DENIS J.
GOTTSBERGER, FRANCIS
GRADY, HON. THOS. F.
GRADY, WALTER L.
GUERTIN, RT. REV. G.A.
GUINEVAN, REV. PETER F.
GUMMERSBACH, JOSEPH
HAGGERTY, J. HENRY
HALLORAN, JOHN H.
HAMILTON, WM. PETER
HANNAN, JOHN
HANNON, LINDLEY A.
HANRAHAN, REV. JAS. V.
HARPER, JOHN J.
HARRINGTON, REV. W. H.
HARRIS, CHARLES N.
HARTFORD, GEO. H.
HAYES, CADY
HAYES, RT. REV. MGR. P. J., V.G.
HEALY, REV. GABRIEL A.
HEARN, REV. DAVID W., S.J.
HEIDE, HENRY

HEIDE, WILLIAM F.
HELLMAN, HENRY
HENDRICK, HON. PETER A.
HENNESSY, D. J.
HERBERMANN, ALEXANDER J.
HERBERMANN, PROF. CHAS. G.
HERBERMANN, HENRY
HERIN, WILLIAM O.
HICKEY, REV. DAVID J.
HICKEY, JOHN J.
HICKEY, REV. JOHN J.
HICKEY, REV. W. D.
HIGGINS, FRANCIS
HIMMEL, REV. JOSEPH, S.J.
HOEY, REV. J. L.
HOFFMANN, THOS. A.
HOLTZMAN, L. F.
HOLWICK, REV. F. G.
HOPKINS, JOHN A.
HOWARD, REV. JAS. J.
HUGHES, REV. J. T.
HUGHES, REV. W. F., D.D.
HUSSEY, J. B.
HURLEY, RT. REV. MGR. EDW. F.
JORDAN, JOHN
JOYCE, MICHAEL J.
KEAN, REV. JOHN J.
KEANE, JAMES R.
KEANE, MOST REV. JOHN J., D.D.
KEARNEY, RT. REV. MGR. JOHN F.

KELLNER, REV. J. A.
KELLY, DR. CHARLES J.
KELLY, MRS. HUGH
KELLY, REV. JOSEPH S.
KELLY, THOMAS H.
KENNEDY, THOS. F.
KENNELLY, BRYAN L.
KENT, JOHN S.
KERESEY, JOHN T.
KIELTY, M. J.
KIERAN, JOSEPH N.
KIERNAN, PATRICK
KING, PERCY J.
KING, WILLIAM R.
KLAUDER, REV. FRANCIS
  E., C.SS.R.
LAFORT, REV. REMY
LAMARCHE, HENRY J.
LAMMEL, VERY REV.
  MGR. ANTHONY
LANE, REV. JOHN I.
LAVELLE, RT. REV. MGR.
  M. J.
LAWLER, JOSEPH A.
LEAHY, JOHN J.
LEARY, THOMAS J.
LENANE, THOMAS
LENNON, REV. JAS. D.
LEONARD, REV. EDW. F.
LEWIS, JAMES M.
LIBRARIAN, BOSTON
  PUBLIC LIBRARY
LINEHAN, PAUL H.
LINGS, VERY REV. A. A.
LIVINGSTON, REV. WM.
LONARGAN, REV. JOHN
  P.
LOUBAT, JOSEPH F.

LUDDEN, RT. REV. P.A.,
  D.D.
LUMMIS, WILLIAM
LYNCH, JAMES
LYNCH, JAMES D.
LYNCH, JAMES F.
LYNCH, DR. J. B.
LYNCH, RT. REV. MGR.
  J. S. M., D.D.
LYONS, JERE C.
MCALEER, REV. P. P.
MCANERNEY, JOHN P.
MCBRIDE, T. J.
MCCAFFREY, JOHN B.,
  M.D.
MCCALL, HON. EDW.
  E.
MCCARTEN, MRS. ELIZ-
  ABETH C.
MCCARTEN, MICHAEL
  K.
MCCLURE, DAVID
MCCLURE, REV. WM. J.
MCCORMACK, FRANK J.
MCCORMICK, JAMES W.
MCCREADY, RT. REV.
  MGR. CHAS. J.
MCCUE, REV. E. J.
MCCUSKER, P. J.
MCDONNELL, RT. REV.
  CHAS. E., D.D.
MCELDERRY, VINCENT
  J.
MCELROY, MRS. WM.
  B.
MCFAUL, RT. REV. JAS.
  A., D.D.
MCFEE, JOHN J., M.D.

McGare, Rev. Thos. F.
McGean, Edward J.
McGean, Rt. Rev. Mgr. James H.
McGolrick, Very Rev. Mgr. Edw. J.
McGovern, James
McGuire, Edward J.
McGuire, Jos. Hubert
McHugh, Rev. John B.
McKenna, Rt. Rev. Mgr. Edward
McKenna, Thomas P.
McLoughlin, Miss Mary J.
McLoughlin, Wm.
McMahon, Rt. Rev. Mgr. D. J.
McMahon, James
McMahon, John B., M.D.
McMahon, Rev. Dr. Joseph H.
McNaboe, James M.
McNamara, Rt. Rev. Mgr. P. J.
McNamee, John
McParlan, Edw. C.
McParland, John E.
McPartland, Stephen J.
Madden, Rt. Rev. Mgr. John T.
Maguire, James D.
Maguire, Rev. Wm. J.
Maher, Rev. J.J., C.M.
Maloney, Martin
Maloney, Maurice T.

Manhattan College
Martin, James J.
Mayo, Hon. John B.
Meany, Edward, M.D.
Meehan, Thomas F.
Meenan, Rev. Wm. B.
Meister, Rev. Isidore
Messmer, Most Rev. S. G., D.D.
Meyer, Rev. Henry J.
Miller, Rev. Wm. C.
Mitchell, John J.
Moffit, William H.
Monks, John, Jr.
Mooney, Rt. Rev. Mgr. Joseph F.
Morrell, Mrs. Edw.
Morris, Rt. Rev. John B.
Morris, Rev. John J.
Mosher, Thomas
Mother Superior, Academy Mt. St. Vincent
Mother Superior, Sisters of Charity
Moynahan, Bartholomew
Moynahan, Thomas B.
Mulgrew, James T.
Mullaly, John
Mullany, Bernard J.
Mullany, Rev. J. F.
Mullen, Rev. J. J.
Mulqueen, Hon. Jos. F.
Mulqueen, Michael J.
Mulry, Thomas M.

Murphy, Edward
Murphy, James J.
Murphy, Miss Nora
Murphy, Very Rev. Mgr. W. G.
Murphy, Rev. Thomas E., S.J.
Murphy, Rev. W. H.
Murray, Charles
Murrin, James B.
Myhan, Rev. Thos. F.
Nageleisen, Rev. J. A.
Neagle, Rev. Richard
Neill, Charles P.
Nolan, James
Nolan, Rev. John A.
Noonan, Rev. James E.
Noonan, John
Norris, Rev. John W.
Norris, Rev. Joseph I., D.D.
O'Brien, Edward J.
O'Brien, Very Rev. F. A., LL.D.
O'Brien, Rt. Rev. Mgr. John
O'Brien, Dr. John J.
O'Brien, Miles M.
O'Brien, Hon. Morgan J.
O'Brien, Thomas S.
O'Callaghan, Rt. Rev. T. A., D.D.
O'Connell, Rt. Rev. D. J., D.D.
O'Connell, John
O'Connor, Harold H.
O'Connor, P.

O'Connor, Rt. Rev. John J., D.D.
O'Connor, Thomas H.
O'Connor, William P.
O'Donoghue, Mrs. Jos. J.
O'Donohue, Louis V.
O'Flaherty, Wm. P.
O'Gorman, Hon. James A.
O'Gorman, Richard J.
O'Gorman, Rt. Rev. Thomas, D.D.
Ohligschloger, J. B.
O'Keefe, Rev. John J.
O'Keefe, Rev. T. M.
O'Keeffe, John G.
Olcott, Mrs. Dr.
O'Leary, Miss Mary
O'Leary, Rev. P. J.
O'Marra, Rev. Pat'k A.
O'Meara, Stephen
O'Neil, Rev. Denis P.
O'Rourke, Jeremiah
Orr, William C.
O'Sullivan, Charles
O'Sullivan, J. D.
Owens, Joseph E.
Pallen, Conde B.
Penny, Very Rev. Wm. L.
Perry, Charles J.
Pettit, Rev. Geo., S.J.
Phelan, Rev. Thos. P.
Philbin, Eugene A.
Prendergast, Jas. M.
Prendergast, Wm. A.

SPILLANE, REV. EDW. P., S.J.

SULLIVAN, J. H.

SUPERIOR, Convent St. Joseph (Brentwood)

SWEENY, REV. EDWIN M.

TAAFFE, VERY REV. MGR. THOMAS

TAAFFE, THOMAS GAFFNEY

TACK, THEODORE E.

TALLEY, ALFRED J.

TAYLOR, REV. MATTHEW A.

TERNAN, GERALD B.

THEBAUD, PAUL G.

THERESA, SISTER· VINCENT

THOMPSON, T. P.

THORNTON, REV. THOS. A.

THUILLE, REV. JOS. M.

TIERNEY, REV. EDW. J.

TIERNEY, HENRY J.

TIERNEY, MYLES

TIERNEY, DR. MYLES J.

TOOHILL, REV. JOHN WILLIAM

TOWLE, P. J.

TRAVERS, VINCENT P.

TREACY, RICHARD S.

TULLY, JAMES M.

VAN ANTWERP, REV. FRANCIS J.

VARNAGIRIS, VINCENT V., Ph.D.

VERDAGUER, RT. REV. PETER, VIC. APOST.

WADE, JOSEPH H.

WALL, RT. REV. MGR. FRANCIS H., D.D.

WALSH, RT. REV. LOUIS S., D.D.

WALSH, RICHARD L.

WALSHE, REV. R. F.

WALTERS, CHARLES F.

WEBBER, CHARLES A.

WEIR, REV. JOHN F.

WHALEN, GROVER M.

WHITE, W. F.

WHITE, DR. WHITMAN V.

WIENKER, VERY REV. H. CLEMENT

WILMER, VERY REV. ANTONINUS, O.M. CAP.

WOODLOCK, THOS. F.,

WOODS, REV. JOSEPH, S.J.

WRIGHT, FRANCIS E.

WUCHER, REV. THEOPHILE, S.M.P.

WYNNE, REV. JOHN J., S.J.

YAWMAN, P. H.

ZWINGE, REV. JOSEPH, S.J.

Lightning Source UK Ltd.
Milton Keynes UK
UKHW020037260219
337881UK00006B/278/P